# The Couch

**The Initial Interview in Psychotherapy**
Argelander, H., M.D.

**Children and Their Parents in Brief Therapy**
Barten, H. H., M.D., Barten, S. S., Ph.D. (eds.)

**Brief Therapies**
Barten, H., M.D. (ed.)

**The Art of Empathy**
Bullmer, K., Ed.D.

**Basic Psychological Therapies**
Fix, A. J., Ph.D. and Haffke, E. A., M.D.

**Assert Yourself!**
Galassi, M.D., Ed.D. and Galassi, J. P., Ph.D.

**The Group as Agent of Change**
Jacobs, A., Ph.D. and Spradlin, W., M.D. (eds.)

**Psychodrama**
Greenberg, I. A., Ph.D. (ed.)

**The Narcissistic Condition**
Nelson, M. C. (ed.)

**Emotional Flooding**
Olsen, P. T., Ph.D.

**The Couch**
Stern, H., Ph.D.

**Psychotherapy and the Role of the Environment**
Voth, H. M., M.D. and Orth, M. H., M.S.W.

**The Therapeutic Self**
Watkins, J. G., Ph.D.

**Clinical Child Psychology**
Williams, G. J., Ph.D. and Gordon, S., Ph.D. (eds.)

**Family Therapy**
Zuk, G. H., Ph.D.

# The Couch

## Its Use and Meaning in Psychotherapy

### Harold R. Stern, Ph.D.

**HUMAN SCIENCES PRESS**
72 Fifth Avenue    3 Henrietta Street
NEW YORK, NY 10011 ● LONDON, WC2E 8LU

Library of Congress Catalog Number 77-15610

ISBN: 0-87705-303-0

Copyright © 1978 by Human Sciences Press
72 Fifth Avenue, New York, New York 10011

Printed in the United States of America
89 987654321

**Library of Congress Cataloging in Publication Data**

Stern, Harold R
   The couch, its use and meaning in psychotherapy.
   Bibliography: p. 201
   Includes index.
   1. Psychoanalysis. I. Title. [DNLM:
1. Psychotherapy—Methods. WM420 S839c]
RC506.S735     616.8'917     77-15610
ISBN 0-87705-303-0

# Contents

*Foreword*                                                        7
  1. Introduction                                               11
  2. Cultural Influences on the Use of the
     Couch                                                      23
  3. The Significance of the Couch in Humor                     39
  4. The Couch as a Symbol of the Posed
     Threats of Psychoanalysis                                 52
  5. The History of the Use of the Couch:
     Developments in Psychoanalytic Theory
     and Practice                                              57
  6. The Theory of Repression as Applied to
     the Couch                                                 74
  7. The Recumbent Position and Its Relation
     to Sleep                                                  86

8.  The Use of the Couch to Facilitate
    Relaxation and the Expression of Feelings    105
9.  Technique in Using the Recumbent
    Position                                     115
10. The Relation of the Couch to the Goals of
    Treatment                                    176
*Appendix*                                       192
*References*                                     193
*Index*                                          211

*Foreword*

This book fills an important gap in psychoanalytic literature. Although the analytic couch has captured the attention of the public at large and is repeatedly referred to in patients' accounts of their personal experience in psychoanalysis, Dr. Stern is the first practitioner to write a book on this most visible and distinctive accoutrement of the analytic situation.

He directs attention to the professional literature that has accumulated on the subject, but this book is much more than a compendium. Comprehensively and creatively, the author pursues the significance and use of the couch in diverse perspectives—in terms of history and cultural influences as well as its bearing on the theory, technique, and goals of psychoanalysis. He suggests guidelines for the use of the couch, illustrating its therapeutic value with clinical material drawn from his own practice and that of colleagues.

The vast range and amazing diversity of human reactions to one object are reflected in the assembled views of scores of psychotherapists on the couch and its clinical use. I am particularly impressed with the numerous meanings acquired by the analytic couch over the many years since Freud introduced it.

Analysts entering practice today tend to take the use of the couch for granted, confirming Dr. Stern's belief that it is insufficiently studied and inadequately understood. But to many practitioners of my vintage who worked in psychiatric hospitals decades ago, the couch has a special meaning. For example, when I conducted analytic therapy nearly 40 years ago in a research-oriented state mental institution, its consulting rooms were equipped only with desks and chairs. Years later, on visiting that institution, I noticed that couches had been installed in these rooms. Their appearance in some mental hospitals symbolized the demise of that era when the analytic approach to emotional disturbances was ostracized by clinical psychiatrists.

Although I recommend that patients lie on the couch, I do not insist that they do so. When they are given the freedom to choose between couch or chair and opt for the former, this is regarded as cooperative behavior. Willingness to lie on the couch when the treatment begins is also of prognostic significance and a clue to the potential duration of the treatment. In general, the patient's attitude toward the couch is a rich source of knowledge about his problems and therapeutic needs.

The sparse consideration given the couch in the professional literature, contrasting sharply with the public's lively interest in it as a symbol of analytic treatment, is difficult to account for. One can only speculate on why the first book on the couch appears just a few years before the centenary of its establishment in the analyst's consulting room. One reason may be that this traditional item of office equipment has commonly been viewed as extraneous to the analytic endeavor. Evidence assembled by Dr. Stern challenges that view and directs attention to the therapeutic significance of the analytic couch as a facilitator of communication.

A basic requirement for personality change through the analytic process is that the patient relive emotionally the originally traumatic situation that produced his psychopathology. Whereas his thoughts, feelings, and memories are likely to be repressed in social situations and even in face-to-face contact with a therapist, when he lies on the couch with the therapist seated behind him he is in the most propitious position for rekindling his impressions of early life. The analytic process involves the communication of all thoughts, feelings, and memories that are active in the patient's mind at a given moment. Those that are associated with psychological disturbances are held in check by forces opposed to free verbal communication (resistance). The pressure to check the reexperiencing and verbalization of thoughts, feelings, and memories of the remote past tends to intensify when the psyche is flooded with stimuli from the external environment. Present sensory experience thus dampens the forces that create transference reactions.

In the context of neurophysiology, the use of the couch makes a unique contribution to the process of exposing the patient to a climate in which transference can develop, can be studied, and can be resolved when it operates as resistance. On the couch, the patient is exposed to less stimulation than if he sat facing the analyst. Because the patient's exteroceptors are less stimulated, his interoceptors gain easier access to the psyche. And with the out-of-sight analyst making a less distinct impression, the patient's previous impressions of other significant objects become more accessible and exert a greater influence on his mind. In this situation, the emotional state that caused the patient's disturbed functioning is eventually recreated in the analytic relationship. In short, by minimizing stimuli that deal with the present and by maximizing stimuli that revive the impressions of past experience, the use of the couch facilitates the communication of emotionally significant material. Thoughts, feelings, and memories of early life have thus become associated with the analytic couch.

For the practitioner sitting behind it and observing the reactivation of the emotional life of patient after patient, the couch becomes a symbol for the infinite variety of human experience.

Hyman Spotnitz, M.D.

# Chapter 1

# INTRODUCTION

Psychoanalysis is perceived with much ambivalence. It is alternately seen as a science and profession that is just beginning to fulfill its potential as an active and beneficial influence, or conversely, one that is on the edge of bankruptcy through lack of interest and positive results (Holt, 1975). These judgments are mostly determined from the vantage point of the observer. If the observer stands outside the mental health profession, he might conclude from the vast number of cartoons, newspaper and magazine articles, novels, and television series that psychoanalysis is the dominant therapy in the mental health field. If the observer is positioned inside the mental health profession, but practices a form of therapy other than psychoanalysis, he might conclude that psychoanalysis is losing its influence because of the proliferation of other therapies with their promise of better, more economical and quicker cures, and the current emphasis upon research, an area where, admittedly, psychoanalysis has problems.

In any event, these various views along with many mis-conceptions obscure the image of psychoanalysis, so that there emerges only a murky picture of the meaning and significance of psychoanalysis for those seeking a simple and clear understanding of this therapy. This is especially true of those who are standing outside of the field.

In sharp contrast to this vague and possibly distorted perception from without, psychoanalysts themselves view their own activities with an almost exaggerated sense of certainty. This sense of certainty seems exaggerated be-cause many of the parameters of psychoanalysis are ques-tioned by most practitioners: the fifty-minute hour, the frequency of sessions, the use of the recumbent position, and the diagnostic categories which are applicable to this form of treatment.

Certainty of procedure can be positive insofar as it stabilizes a science. It can also be positive to the extent that confidence in the efficacy of the technique can result in further development of the theory. Overconfidence, how-ever, can limit scientific creativity. In that circumstance bet-ter results might be obtained from a healthy degree of uncertainty which engenders the type of curiosity that leads to scientific creativity. Rigidity of procedure can be nega-tive when it is a facade for latent hostility toward potentially threatening ideas.

One of the problems in psychoanalysis lies in the area of teaching. Some of the practices in psychoanalysis seem so self-evident, have been ongoing for so long a time, and tend to be verbally passed down unquestioningly from older to younger analysts, that these practices are carried out without much examination, as though they were inher-ited orthodox dogma. To those outside of psychoanalysis the alleged benefits of these practices are not so self-evi-dent. Not all of these practices are fully and rationally ex-plained in psychoanalytic literature, nor are they well understood.

The subject of this book, the use and meaning of the couch in psychoanalysis, is one of those heretofore insufficiently illuminated areas that has been selected for examination and amplification. By exploring the use and meaning of the couch the reader can gain an understanding of how the process of symbolization has seized upon the couch both to obfuscate and highlight its true significance. For the many participants of psychoanalysis, using the couch as a symbol has permitted a shield of insulation to be constructed between the actual process of psychoanalysis and the feelings and thoughts of those threatened by this process. That psychoanalysis can be threatening is a matter of little doubt to those immediately involved in therapy. The nature of this threat is a serious matter and is one of the salient issues discussed here.

For the psychoanalyst, the couch is an ever-present visual reminder and indeed a symbol of his work. Other psychotherapeutic professionals share similar office equipment, but the couch alone distinguishes the analyst's unique experience. The couch has come to play an extremely important role in the analyst's approach to treating patients. Its construction, form, and location in the office, is therefore, a matter of great interest.

Although the clinical use of the couch (and the attendant reclined position) is basic to the practice of orthodox psychoanalysis, it is seldom referred to in the professional literature. This is in strong contradistinction to the frequent references made to it by people outside of the profession. In the public media the couch is almost always mentioned as a symbol connected with the psychoanalytic school of thought or treatment procedure.

Considering how important the couch is in psychoanalytic treatment, it is unfortunate that heretofore there has been little attempt to study all the myriad theoretical and clinical aspects of its use. Early in my psychoanalytic training, I became intrigued by the use of the couch as an object of psychoanalytic treatment. In more recent years I have taken notice of all references to this subject in both the professional and lay literature, and I began to keep a record of ideas I had on the topic. Gradually a number of theoretical issues and their implications emerged.

A review of the rather scant literature on the couch reveals that not a single book on this particular subject exists, and indeed, only six analytic articles have been cited in the recently published literature indexed under couch (Kelman, 1954; Hall and Closson, 1964; Gruen, 1967; Robertiello, 1967; Rosenbaum, 1967; Chessick, 1971).

In pursuing this study a curious and striking paradox becomes evident. The paradox is the tremendous emphasis given to the couch by the public, and the contrasting neglect of the couch from within the profession. This dichotomy between the almost exaggerated attention given the couch in the public media and the paucity of studies in the professional literature must be explained. Why has so little attention been paid to an element in the treatment process that is so integral a part of every psychoanalyst's work? If we select as a probable answer that the subject is of too trivial importance to be considered, we are left with a less than adequate response, for psychoanalytic discipline has taught us that lack of attention to an area of human activity can also be due to the process of denial. As an analyst I am obliged to review the nature of the process of this resistance that operates so forcefully to prevent critical psychoanalytic review of this subject.

Sigmund Freud (1940) provided some clues in suggesting that both exaggerated emphasis and significant omission hinted that something was being avoided. Psychologically, this process can be explained in terms of the mechanisms of denial, displacement, repression, and isolation, all of which implement the process of disavowal.

These mechanisms operate under the following general principles: repression, isolation, displacement, and denial.

Repression is the wholesale rejection from consciousness of certain thoughts and feelings. In his basic formulation of the theory of repression Freud describes the ego's need to regulate and protect the individual from very primitive sexual and aggressive drives and their unconscious disorganizing influences. These drives which exist in all of us are subject to limitation and modification, but not to extinction. The ego encounters these drives when necessary through its invocation of the defensive mechanisms (Anna Freud, 1946b).

Isolation is the detachment of feelings from an idea.

Displacement is the attachment of a thought or feeling to an inappropriate idea or object.

Denial can be a recognition of a thought or feeling, but with a detachment from its real significance. All of these mechanisms tend to protect the individual or the group from contact with certain unacceptable realities (Brenner, 1957).

An incident illustrating the importance of omission is an anecdote the late Theodore Reik (1948) told concerning his quandary on how to treat a patient who said he had nothing to talk about. Freud advised Reik to direct his patient to talk about those things which were least important in his life and least likely to come to his mind or occupy his serious attention. Following Freud's directive, Reik marvelled at the surprising and progressive results that ensued.

Psychoanalysts know that when a topic is avoided, the neglect may be due to the overinvestment of feeling in that area which is repressed in order to avoid the threat of an investigation of these feelings and thoughts. If these thoughts and feelings were to be opened to exploration, painful and frightening reactions might be produced.

Psychoanalytic theory supports a concept of the mind which includes the idea that the ego of the individual is an agency which, through its functions of mediating and structuring cognitive operations including those of perception, memory, judgment, and indeed all reality contacts, regulates the way a stimulus is received and how it will be subsequently acted upon. Several people can consciously band together to protect themselves from a threat that may be real or imagined. In doing so they share and activate in one another similar ego defense mechanisms, i.e., those strategies that the ego has at its disposal to manage and reduce or alleviate perceived emotional threats. Thus, analysts as a group could share certain mechanisms that they might utilize to protect their individual egos and block or change the direction of the drives stimulated in the course of their clinical everyday work with patients.

Sharpe (1950, p. 16) speaks of sublimation as one of the possible expressions of these drives which may be unconsciously at work in the psychoanalyst's defensive system.

> Analysis should have given us the knowledge of why we have become psychoanalysts. We should know the unconscious roots of a major sublimation of this kind. Like other arts, psychoanalysis tends to swamp other interests and encroaches more and more on the time of the whole personality. There are reasons for this, and we do well to know them. We do well to know the deep-seated gratification that we get from the work in order that deep-lying anxieties may be recognized and resolved in their true connections and not superficially explained.

In few other professional activities is it expected that an individual be constantly stimulated by continuous exposure to primitive sexual and aggressive provocations. Most people enter and remain in psychoanalytic treatment because of the frustration and inner unresolved anxiety of their daily lives. As different areas of patients' personality dynamics are systematically explored, the analyst gradually takes on the role of a partner in an emotional growth process. However assiduously he may try, the analyst cannot be an emotionally neutral party to this process. Not only are his feelings and thoughts mobilized, but additionally his defenses against the process are mobilized in a way similar to his or her patients.

It may be potentially overwhelming and unhealthy for the analyst to be completely open to the stimuli directed at him by his patients; however, to be too insulated from these stimuli may make him ineffective and wooden. If the analyst has been both well-trained and well-analyzed and is an emotionally healthy person, the regulatory mechanisms of his or her ego hopefully will allow a proper balance of incoming stimuli and responses to them. The use of the couch assists this process.

The couch, when viewed in the context of a reality-based conscious approach, appears to facilitate the analytic process on behalf of both the analyst and the analysand. The analysand's recumbent position tends to reduce all active and potential motor activity to a minimum. When the patient eventually becomes trained to proscriptively lie on the couch and talk he is insured against anything but the most secure kind of verbal communication. Implicit in the understanding between two parties in the consulting room is the idea: "No matter what I feel, think, say or believe, or you feel or think, I will stay in my place, you will stay in yours, and we will just go on talking together." By such an implied communication, it is believed that the analyst is prepared to be nonjudgmental and nonpunitive without compromising his own sense of values.

We may speculate that for the public, the couch has come to represent what transpires in the psychoanalytic encounter. We may postulate a further conjecture: on an unconscious level it may represent the repressed sexual and aggressive wishes of the psychoanalyst toward himself and his patient. To avoid the anxiety connected with the conflicts these wishes invoke, feelings can be isolated from their sources, real meanings denied, and wishes repressed. These processes can be converted into a symbolic representation such as the couch, which then can stand in the place of what is denied, repressed, or isolated.

For both the public and the analyst, the couch can be a symbol for the conflicts against which the ego defends itself. These conflicts revolve around the basic struggle over sexual and aggressive drives to which civilization is heir (Freud, 1930). The couch or bed is not only the place for sleep where all human activities are at a minimum, but it also represents the ultimate in sexual expression. In English as well as in other languages to take or invite someone to bed is understood to be sexually aggressive. In French, the phrase, "coucher avec quelqu'un" is very explicit in its sexual meaning. Thus it is evident that the psychoanalytic process utilizes as an instrument of technique a piece of furniture that has a possible double (though ambiguous and confused) meaning. An investigation of this process may reveal why the study of the couch has been isolated from the otherwise creative richness of psychoanalysis, for in general the couch is seldom considered in the discussion of theory and technique.

While psychoanalysts utilize the couch as part of their technique, their literature fails to emphasize that the couch is essential to technique. It seems rather to be considered an adjunct to the analytic process. When the symbolic (i.e., primitive) significance of the couch is overlooked and its importance is diminished, a form of rationalization may be operating. Rationalization, another defense mechanism, is a thought process by which the real meaning of a phenomenon is shifted into another meaning, or the value of the meaning is elevated or diminished.

A comprehensive study of this subject necessarily includes an analysis of both social as well as psychological factors. While psychoanalysis as a treatment is limited to the confines of the consulting room, its influence on cultural, political, and intellectual life in general is considerable. A brief survey of the book review pages of newspapers, Sunday supplements, and magazines suggests to the analyst, at least, the tremendous amount of attention psychoanalysis receives in the lay press. Every aspect of our daily lives reflects the influence of psychoanalysis, and inevitably the subject of psychoanalysis is introduced and represented to the public through the medium of the couch.

A historical survey of the origin, development, and meaning of the couch goes hand in hand with a study of the social and intellectual environment in which psychoanalysis initially developed and flourished earlier in this century. Inherent in such a survey is an awareness of the development of the psychoanalytic movement itself.

The psychoanalytic movement like other sciences has experienced some rather stormy times. The theoretical and political foundations upon which psychoanalytic practice is thought to be based have frequently been challenged in ways which threatened to fracture concerned and consensual opinion with regard to certain fundamental, central and critical issues, e.g., the dissonance occasioned by "the question of lay analysis" is an unmistakable example of such a crisis (Freud, 1926; Lorand, 1969).

Although the use of the couch has not been a central theme for protracted theoretical disagreement, some splinter groups, including certain followers of Harry Stack Sullivan (Fromm-Reichmann, 1950), have denied any benefits resulting from the systematic use of the couch as part of the analytic process. Others, such as Karen Horney, although rejecting many of the important tenets of classical psychoanalytic theory and practice, have nevertheless retained the use of the couch (Kelman, 1954).

With few exceptions, previous authors have not explored the ideas and feelings of those party to and intimately involved within the therapeutic alliance. These feelings range from domination to exploitation. While such feelings tend to both feed and discredit the analytic process, they raise the question why, outside of the fairly cohesive views held by psychoanalysts themselves, there should be such a disparity of informed analytic opinion.

Since the couch is believed to be symbolic of psychoanalysis, it is useful to discuss the etiology of that phenomenon. This would require us to examine the social framework within which the psychoanalytic dialogue operates.

The analyst has almost always operated in a socially hostile intellectual climate. Although psychoanalysis is much better understood and accepted than in Freud's early days, contemporary jokes, cartoons, and folk humor indicate much covert, if not blatantly overt hostility directed toward psychoanalysis (and toward those who practice it). It is likely that humor is used to disguise real thoughts and feelings about psychoanalysis. A familiarity with the psychology of humor is relevant to understanding how people can use humor to insulate themselves against the threat of certain conflicts that psychoanalysis can bring to consciousness. The association in the mind of the public between humor and psychoanalysis creates an image that is a combination of and a compromise between what is threatened, what is denied, and what is socially acceptable. The compromise in the form of the couch as a symbol often becomes a basic element of humor whenever psychoanalysis is considered. However, while humor converts that which is potentially threatening (i.e., psychoanalysis) into a form which is quite amusing, the result is a definite negative influence upon certain people who otherwise might have been considering going into therapy. It thus can act as a deterrent to seeking help for vulnerable individuals. Once they approach an analyst for treatment, people are threatened by the sight of the couch because they have so often seen it depicted in a ridiculing and pejorative way. A study of humor, therefore, has merit, as the latent negative feelings fuel part of the resistance initially to seeking treatment, and subsequently to lying willingly on the couch.

Culturally, psychoanalysis operates contrary to many expected methods of direct communication. For example, people expect to look and be looked at when they speak to others. The couch frustrates this expectation. Freud (1913b) openly expressed his objection to being looked at by his patients while they were in treatment. Other analysts also have stated their discomfort at day-long exposure to their patients' disquieting, anxious glances. Because the entire process of looking and being looked at while speaking is such an accepted mode of human communication, the idea of engaging in that different kind of human communication which is peculiar to psychoanalysis inevitably meets with some objection. The dimensions of these objections and how the analyst responds to them deserves a critical and extended examination. These objections come not only from the general public, but also from other professionals.

People outside the profession probably do not realize that psychoanalysis makes up only a very small segment of the field of psychotherapy. Out of an estimated 50,000 full and part-time psychotherapists in the United States, there are perhaps only about 2,500 institute-trained psychoanalysts.* Many psychotherapists are opposed to putting the patient in a recumbent position and see the couch as fostering dependency, regression, and inactivity. Many of these claims are true. The couch does restrain a patient's desire to be active in terms of his own treatment. The possible implications of the recumbent position are frustrating in terms of the wish to "do something." There is,

*Please see Appendix I (Statistical Estimated Analysis of Practicing Professionals Engaged in Psychotherapeutic Disciplines).

therefore, because of this and other issues at conflict, a reasonable challenge to psychoanalysts to better explain their reasons for using the couch.

Psychoanalytic theory not only attempts to explain man's behavior and the motives behind it, but also serves as a foundation for a technique that, if successfully utilized, alleviates an individual's emotional conflicts. Theory as it applies to the couch should explain the general and special dynamics of the supine position and the personality changes such an altered position might prompt. This process works best with an understanding of why certain measures are effective and why others are not. In general, the use of the couch by most analysts is a matter of emulation, rather than an advocation of it bared upon studying and understanding the significant dynamic factors underlying the use of the recumbent position.

A broad investigation of psychoanalysis permits all of the above mentioned elements to be seen in a larger perspective. This book is an attempt to draw together these many diverse ideas. Hopefully the following discussion will encouage new thinking relevant to the use of the couch, a use which should be increasingly based upon a clear and conscious understanding of many of the issues involved.

# Chapter 2

# CULTURAL INFLUENCES ON THE USE
# OF THE COUCH

Psychoanalysis has had a subtle, but undeniable impact on the intellectual currents of the twentieth century. Freud's work has heavily influenced the evolving development of all the social sciences and has been incorporated into the conventional wisdom of our culture and of its institutions.

In turn, the profession of psychoanalysis itself has had to take into consideration the attitudes and expectations of the milieu in which it operates both as a science and as a therapy. Analysts as members of society are consciously and unconsciously aware of the many forces that can affect their work. They must take these into consideration in carrying out their tasks. For example, in continuing the traditional use of the couch, the analyst must deal directly with objections from many patients. Many of them who formerly sat in the audience chuckling with others on the absurdity of the recumbent position and anyone unfortunate enough to have to assume it, are now asked to take this position themselves. They are now requested to be physically passive and verbally active.

The concept of passivity is one to which some attention should be given. Therapists from Asia are often struck by the aggressive behavior toward the therapist by the person in our culture seeking help. And it is often true that the patient is extremely aggressive toward his therapist ("Why don't you help me? You must help me!"), while, in contrast, he is passive in terms of carrying out instructions to cure his illness ("I can't do anything") (Ahsen, 1966).

Kurt Adler (1967, p. 325), the son of Alfred Adler, sees the use of the couch as not only promoting the idea of passivity, but also of inferiority/superiority in the analytic relationship. He writes:

> In line with the need to collaborate in analysis, the ideal situation is for patient and analyst to sit face-to-face, as equal fellow men. Almost all patients feel it to be a position of inferiority to lie on the couch while the analyst sits in lordlike fashion above him. Although transference is enhanced, the development of a genuine human relationship is made virtually impossible by such an unequal position. In psychotic cases, where patients are in desperate need to come to more friendly and accepting terms with reality, the crucial relationship with the analyst as friend and human being is the necessary bond. Lying on the couch does not help at all, but rather enhances unreality. If, however, a patient asks to be allowed to lie on the couch, he should, of course, be permitted to do so, after the reasons for this request are discussed. At the beginning of the analysis, a patient may request this because he is ashamed to reveal certain things while facing the analyst. Each patient of mine who has requested this has, after a short time decided to sit and face me. In all cases the reasons for a face-to-face relationship have to be gone into.

Consistent with this view of therapy, Adler sees the need for providing his patients with a warm and positive relationship as a means of resolving the patient's mental stress. He sees the therapist's function as being a supplier of reality orientation and of providing his client with a bond with another human being. This being the case it is understandable that the supine position would be considered antithetical to progressive treatment. Some psychoanalysts (Spotnitz, 1969) would argue, however, that this approach is not necessarily helpful to the psychotic patient. They would assert that the psychotic person needs to feel and express rage and a too positive approach by a therapist inhibits this expression.

Jungian analysts are also concerned with the psychological position inferred by the analyst looking down on the patient. Gerhard Adler (1967, p. 347) says:

> This technical difference in the external position expresses at the same time a fundamental difference in the whole attitude to the patient. If you sit behind your patients, without coming into view, you assume symbolically a completely unassailable position, that of a superior being over against whom the patient's own personality and worth sink into nothingness; you corner the patient in his neurosis. To sit face to face, on the other hand, is to admit symbolically that the patient is indeed in certain respects ill and in need of treatment, but that nevertheless he himself still exists as an independent entity.

The above statement is inconsistent with many of our cultural assumptions. To sit face to face can be a denial of any element of sickness, while lying down in the presence of another person sitting up can be an acknowledgement of illness. Also, being out of the view of the therapist does not inherently make the patient's personality and worth sink into nothingness. If this should occur, then it is usually the personality of the therapist and the nature of their relationship rather than the physical positioning that is the cause. Most patients who leave psychoanalytic treatment after lying on the couch do so with a superior sense of self worth, a feeling they did not have when they started analysis.

While he ostensibly seeks change, a patient most often really wants his analyst to modify his environment so that he will not have to modify his behavior. Passivity lies behind many of the demands expressed to the therapist: "Get my boss off my back," "Stop my husband from criticizing me," "Make my father give me money." Simultaneously, outside of therapy the patient inevitably engages in forms of activity (acting out), or behavior designed to perpetuate the distress from which he claims to want relief through treatment.

The couch plays a role in a process that tends to reverse the active and passive components of the situation. Entering treatment, the patient is involved in a passive role vis-a-vis his interested but noncommittal therapist, and he is expected to play an increasingly active role in terms of his illness. As the patient becomes more active, eventually he begins to speak about what he thinks, feels, and remembers so that as complete a picture as possible of his conflicts can emerge. Inevitably resistances to this verbalization will become apparent. When these clusters of resistances are skillfully resolved, analysis then permits the patient to feel everything and say everything. Then, as the sources and meaning of his problems come to the surface, they can be understood and worked through.

Our culture teaches us to challenge authority aggressively. If a patient is asked to lie on the couch, he or she may ask, "Why should I do that?" If he recommends that she not cross her legs, she may ask the analyst to explain why.* These attitudes are in contrast to those that tend to prevail

* A purpose of the treatment is to move the patient's understanding to a higher level of awareness and to verbally communicate this newly acquired awareness. If, for example, the crossing of legs is a defense unconsciously against fear of being penetrated, the verbal expression of the fear is a higher level of communication both to the analyst and to the self. It allows the individual to actively protect himself if the threat is real, and to explore the situation and relax if the threat is not real.

in a country such as India where the patient has a very passive, submissive posture towards the therapist with the belief that any and each of the therapeutic instructions are in the interests of the cure the patient seeks. It would be rare for the therapist to be asked to explain why he does what he does (Ahsen, 1966). Thus, the patient's challenge to the psychotherapist in our culture is in direct contradiction to the usual passive submission to a physician's prescriptions, even though the use of the recumbent position in connection with a treatment activity may also have special therapeutic significance. Most patients leaving the doctor's office are not aware of what has been written on the prescription sheet, yet they demand explanations for the psychotherapist's use of the couch.

This may be explained by the attitude of open and direct challenge, especially toward a figure of authority, which is so prevalent in our society. It may be an outgrowth of distrust existing between parent and child. Those patients we see often have a lightly concealed readiness to express hostility verbally toward their parents, both inside and outside the treatment situation. It is therefore not surprising that similar overt defiant and mistrustful attitudes are carried into the treatment situation and directed at the analyst.

Frequently accompanying this defiant attitude of "Prove it to me" is a belligerent passivity, meaning "Do it for me." After he explains to the therapist what is wrong, i.e., his symptoms, the patient is then prepared to await the prescription for the cure from the therapist. The psychoanalytic process runs counter to these expectations. It is the patient who does most of the talking and ultimately produces the information that leads to the prescription for his own cure. When the treatment goes successfully, the patient learns to be passive in his physical posture on the couch and active in the manner and scope of his talk.

While the analyst may wish for a more cooperative

reaction from his patient, these challenges do not necessarily pose a liability. They can be viewed as conflicts to be studied and understood as resistances, thus leading to the resolution of the neurosis. The suggestion to use the couch can act as a catalyst in this process, for it can more quickly strip away the superficial cover of cooperation which disguises angry defiance in the patient. Working through defiance as a resistance leads to the possibility of real cooperation, without which the analysis cannot reach a healthy conclusion.

## CULTURAL EXPECTATIONS FRUSTRATED BY THE COUCH

In taking the recumbent position, the analysand is reduced to physical passivity. In addition, he must for a time abandon the usual alertness to the behavior of others about him that our culture requires. We have been trained to take an aggressive "eyeball to eyeball" posture when it comes to relating to others. Most people prefer to look at the person to whom they are talking. Consequently, they feel awkward and vulnerable speaking to someone out of sight. An exception to this is the increasing use of the telephone as a nonvisual channel of communication. Most people are fairly comfortable speaking on the phone to someone they cannot see. Yet, on the telephone few people are known to complain "I feel like I am talking to the wall" as they are commonly known to do when first asked to lie on the couch.

Nevertheless, it would be a mistake to believe that even though the analyst is out of sight, he is out of the patient's mind. The slightest sound, either breathing or stirring in the chair, can have deep meaning for the person on the couch. The sight of the analyst at the start of the hour can set the pace for the rest of the session.

That one person observes and the other person is observed has important implications for therapy. These views are well presented by Bateson and Ruesch (1951, p. 271–272):

> In illustration, it is worth mentioning a curious detail in which the strictly Freudian analysis session differs from the majority of the two person systems. When the patient is on the couch and the analyst sits on a chair behind the patient's head, the analyst gets a fair, but perhaps sufficient view of the postures and facial expressions of the patient, but the latter is cut off from seeing his therapist. The asymmetries which this arrangement introduces into the therapy situation are undoubtedly very complex and surely vary from therapist to therapist and from patient to patient. From the point of the present discussion, it is significant that the patient receive only verbal messages from the analyst and so has the maximum freedom to build up a fantasy picture of the affective aspects of the analyst's personality. This picture may be later examined when the transference is analyzed. At first the patient according to lifetime habit, attempts to make inferences about the analyst in order to tailor his words to fit that person. Later he discovers, perhaps, that in the therapeutic session such tailoring is difficult and he is then thrown back upon speaking and acting as "himself" with minimal aid from such introjected images.

Here too, we can see that the emphasis on introjection, projection, and eventually regression (in terms of the transference) may occur as a feature more characteristic to the supine position than to the usual confrontation between two people. The couch is a valuable adjunct in helping the patient express all his thoughts and feelings that are invested in earlier unresolved conflict situations.

## BASES FOR THE ANALYST'S UNSEEN POSITION

Looking at someone or being looked at has much importance so far as the patient is concerned; it likewise possesses considerable significance for the analyst. Many critics of psychoanalysis and the so-called cult which surrounds it point to Freud as a pied piper who plays a melody to which all analysts dance. They state that the psychoanalysts who followed him are emulating the master whose preference for the use of the sofa involved a personal idiosyncracy, a distaste at being looked at.

Coltrera and Ross (1967, p. 44) discuss Freud's attitude to being looked at as follows:

> Taking up the question of the ritual of the couch as against sitting up, he related that in the early days it was especially humiliating to American patients, dating the ceremony to the days of hypnosis and to his own personal dislike for being stared at for long periods of time. However, these are extrinsic sides to the fact that lying on the couch facilitates free rein of thought. The reclining position prevents the patient from "reading" the face of the analyst and from impairing the development of transference.

Freud was a sensitive student of his science and a psychotherapist par excellence, and perhaps his view reflects something of the character of an analyst, his very nature and aptitude for his work.

Eisendorfer (1959, p. 376) writes:

> Perhaps the core of psychoanalytic aptitude in the male resides in his psychologically accessible latent femininity and his correlated passivity. It is this component of his personality that contributes to his capacity to wait and listen while the unconscious of the patient is striving to be born into consciousness. The aggressive masculine tendency "to be doing" must be subordinated to this passive capacity to listen and understand.

This observation of the component personality trait of accessible latent femininity may assist us in comprehending the analyst's aversion to being looked at for long periods of time, and what this aversion means. For one thing, it can be symptomatic of a conflict between the active and passive aspects of his personality. If this conflict remains un-resolved, the analyst is inclined to bury it. For him, out of sight can be out of mind. On the other hand, in a vis-a-vis situation, people must continually work to manage their aggressive impulses. If the analyst has to control his facial expressions, he may become distracted and tired. He does not necessarily want the patient to respond to his face or his gestures, and the use of the couch facilitates these wishes by denying the patient visual feedback.

Otto Fenichel (1945) maintains that shame is a motive for defense directed against exhibitionism, and scopto-philia is the basis for not wanting to be looked at, i.e., "I feel ashamed" means "I do not want to be seen." Shame can be connected with the analyst's guilt feelings. Like any-one else he can think and feel things that he would prefer not be revealed. According to Fenichel (1945), persons who feel ashamed hide themselves.

Exploring the analyst's aversion to being looked at Greenson (1967, p. 399) says:

> Another characteristic of psychoanalysis which distinguishes it from all other psychotherapies is its special emphasis on structuring the relationship between patient and therapist so as to further the development of the transference neuro-sis. In order to facilitate the growth of the neurotic transfer-ence reactions it is necessary that the analyst conduct himself in a way that is different from all other patient-therapist relationships. I am referring here to what may be expressed in shorthand as the depriving-incognito behavior of the psychoanalyst. This leads us to question: What moti-vations might impel a man to seek a career in a field where one of his major tasks is to comport himself in a relatively nonresponsive blank screen to the patient so that the patient can project and displace onto that screen the unresolved and warded-off imagos of the past?
>
> This aspect of psychoanalytic technique seems to come easily to some analysts who indicate a proclivity for isolation, withdrawal, and uninvolvement. Difficulties arise when these analysts are not able to change their attitudes and

technique when the situation calls for it. It has been impressive to me to find so many analysts who are timorous and uncomfortable during the initial interviews because they have to sit face to face with the patient. They tend to cut down on the number of preliminary interviews in order to reach the safety and comfort of their position behind the couch as quickly as possible. Analysis of candidates in training with similar problems reveals they suffer from a form of stage fright which covers repressed exhibitionistic impulses and a generalized aggressivization and sexualization of looking and being seen. The position behind the couch offers them the opportunity to look without being seen.

Ella Freeman Sharpe (1950) shows that the analyst, by the very choice of occupation, wants to look into the patient's mind. He wants to "rummage" there as a form of unconscious gratification aimed at nullification of personal anxieties. However, in a more conscious form, "looking for the patient can be the partial acting out of an erotic transference" to which the analyst is asked to make some response. For valid therapeutic as well as theoretical reasons, the analyst may therefore not want to be stared at, let alone suffer the resulting fatigue of the counter-transference response to being under continued visual surveillance.

Quoting Sharpe (1950, p. 21) "The couch position gives greater ease and freedom to the patient and to the analyst too. The more freely the analyst can listen, the more easily analysis can proceed." Knapp (1954, p. 186) has made a study of the use of the ear:

> The act of listening, then, contributes to superego and ego functions and to instinctual gratification. It remains subordinate to the main sensory representative of reality, vision but extends its bounds. We keep an "eye to the future" to make our major plans, but we have our "ear to the ground" to detect nuances and reverberations. The ear can function as a tentacle, plucking pearls from the sea of words and exploring depths that vision does not reach.

The ear also serves as a more passive vehicle. We offer it as such when we "lend an ear," and we suffer it as such when our ears are filled or "split" by noise. In metaphor, verbal seeds can germinate and grow in it. To "whisper a word" to someone can signify implanting an idea—or, in slang "putting a bug in his ear."

## CULTURAL CONSIDERATIONS IN THE USE OF TECHNIQUE

The ultimate task of the analytic process is resolving the emotional conflicts within the patient. The analytic process must be economic, socially acceptable, and technically efficacious. The use of the couch facililates the process.

Psychoanalytic technique utilizes and extends theory to bring about emotional change or development in the individual. Because psychoanalytic theory considers certain physical, cultural, and environmental factors as beneficial to emotional growth, utilization of these factors in the treatment situation should be part of the technique. We may mention to illustrate this relationship between theory and technique a method of childbirth introduced by a French obstetrician, Leboyer (1973) by which infants are born into semi-darkness because he wants their eyes to grow progressively accustomed to outside light. He believes the infant's emotional growth is enhanced by a benign postpartum experience. The baby is pulled from the mother gently while the doctor strokes it and whispers; all noises are kept at a minimum. Apparently many mothers have claimed that these children are happier, less afraid of life, and are more relaxed than their siblings born in the more typical way.

It is interesting that in many ways the semi-darkness of the psychoanalytic consulting room and the relaxing of the patient in the recumbent position creates a setting which it is hoped will facilitate a rebirth of the patient's personality in a progressive way. It may be that Freud chanced upon this technique through his familiarity with hypnosis before any theory was fully developed (Waelder, 1964).

Ferenczi (1956, p. 187), Freud's close associate, in many ways anticipated Leboyer: He used his analytic insight to describe an ideal postbirth experience for the infant:

> They lay him down by the warm of the mother, or wrap him up in soft, warm coverings, evidently so as to give him the illusion of the mother's warm protection. They guard his eye from light stimuli, and his ear from noise, and give him the possiblity of further enjoying the intra-uterine absence of irritation, or, by rocking the child and crooning to him monotonously rhythmical lullabies, they produce the slight and monotonously rhythmical stimuli that the child is not spared even in utero (the swaying movements of the mother when walking, the maternal heart-beats, the deadened noise from without that manages to penetrate to the interior of the body).

A technique applicable to the theory would consider that semi-darkness, a relaxed prone physical position, the absence of visual orientation to another person, and a quiet environment, not only tends to replicate the post-birth process at its best, but also maximally stimulates the possibilities for emotional reconstruction and growth in any human being with the benign assistance of a surrogate mother, the analyst.

Another possible reaction to providing a setting of this kind is to foster regression, a falling back emotionally to an earlier way of relating to the environment. Although from the analyst's point of view this regression is advantageous to his purpose, the patient will naturally resist this procedure. He has been emotionally and culturally conditioned to avoid situations where he can be perceived as helpless or passive in any way analagous to an infant. This reluctance or fear must in some people be resolved before treatment can comfortably proceed.

Before stepping into the consulting room some prospective patients have a positive expectation of psychoanalysis which will include the use of the couch. This expectation may have been fostered by having heard friends describing their own treatment, by viewing television programs and films, by reading popular novels, or (most commonly) by seeing cartoons about psychoanalysis which invariably show the patient on the couch. When he is invited to make use of the couch, he may demur momentarily, but unless he has some specific conflict concerning the reclining position, he usually will cooperate. After some initial discomfort, the patient accepts the couch as part of the treatment process. If the treatment has a favorable outcome, the patient's regard for the analyst and his technique will likely be positive. The couch can be a symbol of this favorable outcome.

## Symbolic Meanings of the Couch

Just as the shiny relector on the doctor's forehead brings to mind the ear, nose and throat doctor, the black rubber-headed hammer the neurologist, and the scalpel the surgeon, the psychoanalyst is known by his office couch. So well known is the use of the couch to suggest psychoanalysis that an analytic writer, Spotnitz (1961) called his book *The Couch and the Circle*, the circle representing group therapy, and the couch representing psychoanalysis. Another writer, Moser (1977) titles an autobiographical sketch of his own psychoanalytic treatment, *Years of Apprenticeship on the Couch*. A further example of the couch having symbolic meaning is Little's (1967) description of the analysis of a patient who, after seeing a live spider in the therapist's office, expressed symbolic similarities between the spider and his web and the analyst and his couch. Moser (1977) also illustrates how the couch can represent the analyst.

In selecting an object or image to stand for a method, an idea, or a profession, we are applying a natural law: the law of symbolism, Circot (1962). Symbolism is undifferentiated from the entire fabric of human communication, and is, in fact, the very fiber of it. Our earliest forms of written language, cuneiform and hieroglyphics, are symbolic representations of words. The letters of our alphabet stand symbolically for the sounds of our spoken communication: the written word is a symbol for what it represents.

Gerhard Adler (1967, p. 343), a follower of Carl Jung, makes explicit the perception of the couch as a symbol:

> The pros and cons of couch and chair have often been discussed and are, therefore, well known. They have almost become symbols of attitude for analysts. The couch, with the analyst sitting behind the patient, clearly aims at establishing as far as possible (I don't believe it is very far in actual fact) an "impersonal," "objective" analyst figure. That it also forms one of the defense mechanisms used by analysts for self-protection is evident, as is its importance for the counter-transference. The reasons for the couch are well-enough-known to be mentioned only in passing: the freedom of the patient to use the analyst for his transference fantasies, the creation of a "dependent" position facilitating the emergence of infantile material, assisting relaxation and an attitude conducive to free association, and so forth. The couch may also allow the patient to develop a kind of intellectual detachment from his unconscious material; but all these special considerations, which in any case will vary with the type of patient, are secondary to the basic principle underlying the use of the couch or armchair. This is that the chair gives expression to a greater flexibility in the analytical situation.

Symbolization is the unconscious process by which certain emotional values are displaced from one object to another. Thus, repressed wishes may achieve some measure of disguised satisfaction, i.e., the unconscious mind which is bypassed remains ignorant of the fact that symbols have been employed.

Freud shows their importance in psychological processes. He explains that certain symbols are doorways through which unconscious ideas are allowed conscious expression, by offering something more socially acceptable to stand for repressed unacceptable thoughts or ideas (Freud, 1900). We can view symbols in the Freudian sense of the term as having economic, topographical, and dynamic characteristics. Economic, in the sense that the choice of symbol is one that can provide the repressed thought or idea with the greatest cathexis (or emotional charge) under the most socially acceptable circumstances. The symbol has a topographical function with many loci of meaning because it has significance on unconscious, preconscious, and conscious levels. In Freud's later formulations the symbol can also be explained in terms of ego, id, and superego. The object symbolized has dynamic aspects when the unconscious part of the object strives toward consciousness, despite continuing inhibitory processes of the ego or superego.

Topographically, not all meanings of the couch are necessarily of deep unconscious levels. Many are near the surface. For example, to think of psychoanalysis in terms of the couch provides a convenient handle by which to grasp more easily a larger group of concepts. Many people, on learning that a person is a psychotherapist, ask, "Do you have a couch?" When there is doubt about his work, linking the man to the couch establishes the kind of therapy he provides. On this level the couch also serves the same function as an abbreviation serves in writing, namely as a shortcut.

Unlike such objects as bookstands or ashtrays, the analytic couch is dynamic in its constant play of meanings.

These meanings for which the couch serves as agent are continually striving for expression. For this reason, it will frequently appear in the dreams and fantasizing of both patients and therapists. This helps explain why the couch is such a popular and ready subject of humor in cartoons and jokes. Simply the idea of a couch is sufficient to produce anger in some people and ridicule in others.

Just as a flag, the symbol of one's country, acts as an object of regard and emotional stimulus, so too the couch as a symbolizing agent comes to be the recipient of attitudes toward its symbolic object: psychoanalysis. We are therefore compelled to study the couch for the subject matter which it represents, that is, psychoanalysis itself. Over the years it has come to represent not only the posture of the patient in psychoanalytic treatment, but also psychoanalysis as a way of thinking about mental and social problems.

Of Harper's 36 systems of psychotherapy, only two or three utilize the recumbent position, only a few are nondirective, and a few deal with mental processes we call "unconscious" (Harper, 1959). Psychoanalysis alone specializes in these three areas. Despite its minority position in terms of numbers of therapists and patients, psychoanalysis draws a disproportionately large amount of lay and professional attention. Discussions about psychoanalysis as a form of therapy appear almost daily in popular journals and magazines.

To other mental health professionals, psychoanalysis may represent an approach to treatment that often seems antithetical to the understanding of the human mind and the emotional disorders. Those opposed to psychoanalysis almost without exception seize upon the use of the couch as a feature of their criticism.

# Chapter 3

# THE SIGNIFICANCE OF THE COUCH IN HUMOR

Humor has a direct relationship to symbolism. Humor, like symbolism, involves the concentration of many things or meanings into a single effective form that is brief yet meaningful. From an economic standpoint, the process of condensation (where the couch is treated as the agent of psychoanalysis, and thus receives in its stead scorn and ridicule), enables a form of attack that is more socially acceptable. By dealing with the couch rather than with psychoanalysis itself, a focusing of many attitudes becomes possible. The final product of this concentrating process involves a compromise between various socially intolerable ideas about psychoanalysis which are striving for expression and those ideas which are acceptable to a group superego.

In studying the technique of jokes, Freud (1905b) discovered many characteristics of the process of humor. Among these was the variety of meanings attached to a word or image as symbol. He shows that though disguise, unconscious tendencies are hidden by double meanings. The double meaning of the couch is (1) a furnishing for reclining and (2) a symbol of psychoanalysis. As a symbol of psychoanalysis the couch offers itself as a target for every accusation aimed at psychoanalysis. These unconscious tendencies are directed toward various kinds of instinctual gratification. Freud (p. 22) says,

> We can understand what it is that jokes achieve in the service of their purpose. They make possible the satisfaction of an instinct (whether lustful or hostile) in the face of an obstacle that stands in its way. They circumvent this obstacle, and in this way draw pleasure from a source which the obstacle had made inaccessible.

He (p. 24) writes further,

> A joke will allow us to exploit something ridiculous in our enemy which we could not, on account of obstacles in the way, bring forward openly or consciously: once again then, the joke will evade restrictions and open sources of pleasures that have become inaccessible. It will further bribe the hearer with its yield of pleasure into taking sides with us without close investigation, just as on other occasions we ourselves have often been bribed by an innocent joke into over-estimating the substance of a statement expressed jokingly.

The obstacles that Freud refers to are open and direct expressions of aggression. The following joke will illustrate some of these principles:

> Having been told by her family doctor that her problem is emotional, an attractive young lady raps on the psychiatrist's door. He admits her and asks her to remove all her clothes and lie on the couch. The doctor then joins her on the couch and enjoys himself with her sexually. Finally, he says, "Well, that takes care of my problem; now tell me yours."

This joke, which usually produces much laughter, illustrates a number of principles of the mechanism of jokes
which we can examine with respect to the couch. When the
attractive young woman is asked initially to undress and lie
on the couch, the situation immediately raises the issue of
sex. When the couch is a piece of furniture ancillary to the
presumed function of medically examining her, the request
that the woman lie on the couch is not unprofessional for
a psychiatrist, since the couch now becomes an accomplice
to the sexual exploitation of the patient. In itself the use of
the recumbent position is strongly suggestive of sexual
action. The couch in this joke is the symbolic bed upon
which the doctor's lust and hostility to the woman is
brought to fruition. Laughter is triggered because the psychoanalyst is preconsciously expected to take advantage of
a situation like this, and we laugh at the confirmation of our
expectation. These expectations, of course, only fulfill in
direct form our own unconscious wishes. Grotjahn (1957,
p. 18) writes:

> Increasing demands for repression through the ages have
> changed aggression from assault into wit. Where we would
> have struck a person in earlier times, we restrict our hostility
> now and often repress it entirely. Aggressive wit gives us a
> new way of admitting dangerous aggression to our con-
> sciousness—but it has to be done in cleverly disguised form.

What Grotjahn says here of aggression also generally applies to sexuality.

Just as humor is evoked by verbal jokes, so too is it
aroused by cartoons, which have more popular and frequent use (Hirsch, 1968). In the cartoon the couch is an
even more condensed symbol, since it has visual impact
and its effectiveness depends on instant recognition of the
couch representing psychoanalysis. We can observe popular beliefs toward psychoanalysis by studying cartoons. A
description of a cartoon may help to illustrate this:

*Cartoon Setting*: The therapist, a bald middle-aged man with glasses, is sitting behind the couch and is perpendicular to it. He is busily writing on his pad. In lieu of a patient on the couch, a tape recorder resting there is playing.

*Dialogue*: The tape recorder saying, "Being a very busy man. . . ."

*Meaning*: Therapy here is a one-way street whereby the patient speaks to the therapist through a tape recorder.

The therapist is a naive fool who mechanically proceeds as if the tape recorder were a person. This is a very depersonalized relationship. Psychoanalysis here is a relationship between two people who have no regard for and no influence on each other. Usually it is the patient who is emotional and the analyst who is cold. Here the situation is reversed. The notebook so often shown on the doctor's lap is an anachronism which is actually seldom used. Part of the humor is due to exposure of the preconsciously expected dehumanization of patients by psychoanalysis. In sum: (1) visiting a psychoanalyst is a waste of time, and (2) of the two involved in psychoanalysis, the therapist is the crazier.

These statements made by a cartoon are understood by means of condensation, disguise, double-meanings, etc.; they are not ordinarily stated openly. Seldom is psychoanalysis openly accused of imposing sexual relations on patients or dehumanizing them. The very sophisticated introjects of the superego in the form of censor do not allow such direct statements of sexuality and aggressiveness. Hostile jokes, cartoons, television skits, and plays lift repression, circumvent the superego, and indirectly open up otherwise inaccessible sources of expression and enjoyment.

All of these theories of wit provide evidence that humor has much of its appeal in areas of suppressed sexuality and hostility that are suddenly given the possibility of expression by a joke or cartoon.

One concept of the analytic situation as an inner sanctum arises from the expectation that whatever goes on inside the doctor's office is very private and secret. The outside world is excluded. This exclusion is in itself capable of evoking powerful fantasies of what could occur in such a private situation, including sexual activity.

The idea that the person behind the helpless victim on the couch can be a potential aggressive threat also adds to the humor. The obvious anal suggestiveness of having someone sitting at the rear can release nervous laughter. The imaginative opportunities for a "goose" are infinite. When some men and women patients were questioned about why the hestitated to lie down they reluctantly explained that they were fearful of being molested or raped.

Another difficulty is that people cannot help drawing the parallel between the doctor as a psychotherapist and the doctor as a medical/physician practitioner. While visiting a doctor, physical handling is expected and acceptable; a visit to an analyst with his use of the couch suggests sexuality. The idea of the analytic situation as sexual is really not acceptable to the superego and therefore is more readily a topic for humor than outright expression. Because of the regularity and frequency of the visits and the use of a couch, the analytic session is even more capable of arousing lover/mistress images. Also, the privacy of the analytic situation is accompanied by indications of unconditioned benevolence with strong potentials for intimacy.

The suspicious fears of what psychoanalysis is all about creates many tensions. Aristophanes' play, *The Clouds,* may have been the first representation of these tensions connected with the use of the couch (Halpern, 1963): the sexual humor it probably evoked to release tensions in ancient Greece is likely still operative today.

There is certainly humor surrounding the idea of a person of any sensibilities lying on the couch and talking to someone behind him. In itself, the recumbent position for communications seems ludicrous. It contradicts all the expected forms of social interchange in a talking relationship. Since talking often serves as socialization rather than communication, it is incongruous that one person reclines while the other sits up out of sight.

The possibility of humor in such an arrangement would disappear if hypnosis were involved. Hypnosis makes the situation resemble an operative procedure with the physician directing and the person on the couch responding to a structured set of events. What seems funny in analysis is that two people should relate to each other consciously from such absurd positions; it is this absurdity that is reflected in humor.

A further source of humor is the concept of a person voluntarily lying on a couch, physically on display, in the full sight of another person. It is embarrassing and dissonant. It could indicate a lack of seriousness on the patient's part. Something about the picture makes it appear as if the patient is talking to himself. In our culture, talking to oneself is considered odd. Repeatedly patients are heard to exclaim, "I feel like I am talking to the walls, like no one is listening."

Much of the humor of the psychoanalytic situation also comes from a certain paradox that the psychotherapeutic experience presents to those generally uninformed about its process. This contradiction has its roots in the development of medicine. By the time of Hippocrates, the function of the physician in western civilization had emerged as quite distinct from that of the faith healer. The faith healer and his patients functioned under the aegis of the priesthood while medicine developed a separate identity.

As a 36-year-old neurologist, Freud had his patients lie on a couch while he practiced hypnotherapy (Kline, 1958). When he abandoned that technique he still adhered to the use of the couch and made the recumbent position its trademark. This was not his intention. Apparently, he never specifically prescribed its use, but rather its employment was due to the tendency of his followers to emulate him. The exploration of the unconscious did not begin with Freud either, but he utilized them both to effect a cure.

When Freud appeared on the Vienna medical scene in the 1890s, his former colleagues' outrage at his "far out" ideas was voiced in explicit charges of quackery. He had, after all, in adopting his new path abandoned most of their concepts regarding the etiology of mental illness. Since Freud's cure started with understanding of his patients, and since this understanding stemmed from really listening to them, many concepts about the relationship of the physician and his patients were turned upside-down. It is normally the doctor who talks to his patient once the symptomatology is conveyed. The idea of spending so much time with one patient was considered equally absurd.

The idea of the doctor who could cure by passively listening is contrary to the usual expectation of curing by "doing something." Every therapist who limits his activity with patients to understanding them, and when necessary, explaining (rather than "doing" something for them) contends with this resentment and lack of comprehension. Even back during the time of Socrates, a patient could laugh at the idea of a physician trying to "fool" him into believing he could cure with words. He would think it a waste of time. It is analogous to the skepticism with which today's public regards the competence of religious leaders in the use of medication. Both situations contain the same elements—a trick is being played with the potential for release of nervous laughter when the ruse is revealed and the trickster exposed. There is hostility directed at the trickster, or his counterpart, the analyst, for his attempts at deception.

Many present-day cartoons reveal patients letting themselves be fooled by analyst, and therefore, ridiculed. Possibly the only other profession similarly the object of so much ridicule is politics. However, in that case, the politician alone, not the voter, is the object of humor while in psychiatric jokes, the therapist, the setting including the couch, and the patient or patients (in the case of group therapy), all are ridiculed. Fritz Redlich (1953, p. 16) has written: "Over the last twenty years, in popular magazines, there has been a steadily increasing number of cartoons and jokes portraying the psychiatrist as exaggeratedly hateful, stupid, venal, sexy or crazy."

A study of the following cartoons elucidates these attitudes on the part of the public:

> *Cartoon Setting*: A stiff, squelched-looking patient lies on an old fashioned, thick, high-end couch. Beside him a bespectacled vapid-looking psychotherapist, with writing pad on his lap, sits on a modern swivel chair to the rear of the couch and faces away from it. There is a diploma on the wall.
>
> *Dialogue*: Patient "I'm getting only twenty-two miles to the gallon in my Volkswagon."
>
> *Meaning*: Both of these fellows are crazy and dumb to be wasting time like this. The old-fashioned couch stands in contrast to the new executive chair as a suggestion of exploitation. The patient goes to rags while the analyst goes to riches.

It often appears to an observer, at first glance, that psychoanalysis runs counter to the development of mature relationships. One person lying on a couch relating to another sitting upright seems congruent to a parent–child relationship, rather than an adult-to-adult relationship. It suggests certain attitudes of adult/child, superior/inferior, dominant/dominated, and creates in general an idea of the person on the couch as quite dependent. The following cartoon illustrates this:

> *Cartoon Setting*: Two executive-type men are walking past a shop window that sells greeting cards. A window placard says, "Don't forget Mother's Day."

*Dialogue*: One of the two briefcase-carrying men looks at his watch and exclaims, "Holy mackerel, I missed my 4 o'clock appointment with the analyst!"

*Meaning*: There is an obvious link between the Mother's Day placard and the patient's realization that his appointment with his analyst has been forgotten. It alludes to a common belief that analysts inculcate a preoccupation to the point of absurdity with the patient's parents, so that the cartoon character cannot think of his mother without thinking of his analyst at the same time. It further suggests that the analyst has conditioned the patient to think of himself as a child and the analyst as a parent.

In a survey of psychiatric jokes, Borosen and Ginsburg (1967) described them as falling into five categories: that (1) psychiatrists are mad, (2) money-hungry, (3) cruel, (4) sex-mad, or that (5) patients who go to them are mad. Reviewing psychiatric jokes, Borosen notes, "Of the 500 or so cartoons and jokes about psychiatrists I've tracked down, there are only a few that seemed favorable." He says these unfavorable attitudes toward psychiatry need not be totally construed negatively and quotes Dr. Fritz Redlich (pp. 417, 426) as stating:

> From the psychiatrist's point of view, the increasing number of cartoons depicting and deriding psychiatry should be welcomed . . . Psychiatrists have gained a status of respect and authority which is reduced in the unmasking process of caricature.

To the extent that cartoons and jokes discharge hostility that has been built up toward psychotherapy, they serve a helpful function. However, the mechanism is not as simple as this. Most of these jokes and cartoons originate in the media centers of large cities, such as New York, where the *New Yorker* is published or Chicago, where *Playboy* is created. These centers set the pace for many areas of culture around the rest of the country from fashions to the theater. Because most people have no knowledge of psychiatry, they do not laugh when they are first confronted with those jokes and cartoons. It is only after the idea and setting is established in their minds that these cartoons take on a humorous quality. In other words, jokes, cartoons, and stories are actually teaching the public a distorted version of psychotherapy.

One should not consider all of this criticism as misdirected. In order that humor be effective there is likely to be some basis in fact, otherwise the reader would not react so willingly. The steady stream of antipsychoanalytic humor would suggest there is a continuing complaint against psychoanalysis. This complaint is not along the same lines of the early reactions to psychoanalysis as it was when Freud introduced his new psychology. Freud was not accused of providing a treatment that was exploitative of the idle rich who wanted to waste their money, as some of the current humor suggests. Neither was he castigated for neglecting social and health needs of the times. Furthermore, psychoanalysis was not then considered part of the establishment as it is today considered the "in" thing.

In examining recent humor we observe that it is far less frequently suggested that psychoanalysis is sex-obsessed than it was in its beginnings. There are other faults indicated in these humorous views of psychoanalysis which may have at least a grain of truth. For example, much of the humor we examine suggests that psychotherapists are ineffectual people. There being a large and bewildering array of therapies available for the public to deal with, the process of simplication and condensation which makes humor possible is further aided by making psychoanalysis the scapegoat for what is good and bad about all therapies. This is evidenced by the fact that while there are probably no more than about 2,500 psychoanalysts in the United States (See Appendix I). Despite this, most cartoons show a couch and imply that what is happening in the psychotherapy is psychoanalytic treatment.

The couch in its use as an adjunct to therapy is evidently a puzzle. People ask, "Why should the couch be an integral part of the treatment process and what difference does it make if you sit up, stand up, or lie down? How can this make sense? Freud started the whole thing, and people think that like sheep, most of his followers have their patients lie on the couch and talk not because of any therapeutic merit, but because Freud's followers are stupid!" This, then, is often a common mode of thinking in regard to the couch.

In terms of basic health needs no real remedy has been found for the treatment of large numbers of people, particularly poor lower class citizens who need treatment. No really effective therapy is available for drug addiction and alcoholism. The question is asked: What does psychotherapy cure? A humorous answer would be: "People with excess money to spend and time to waste." It is suggested that many ills could be better and more cheaply remedied with common sense which, it is implied, analysts lack.

A number of patients were asked to explain this popular poking fun at psychiatry, how it affected them and the way they adjusted to using the couch. Some of the responses were:

> I would feel silly if I were just beginning. In fact, I still feel foolish because of the way that the public looks at it. There are these cartoons and when you see things written, they make fun of it. Also you read that psychoanalysis is passé! There are quicker ways to do it. Now it makes me angry to read this stuff, although some are funny—like this Wee Winnie Winkle. This guy is depicted as a complete fool, a worthless fool.

> I think that a lot of people know they are in trouble and this is a possible way they could help themselves, yet most people know it takes a long time and costs money and they would have to talk about a lot of difficult things. This humor and ridicule is a defense against something they don't want

to feel. Like my first doctor. When I first saw him, I was so satisfied over the fact that he was a creep. It confirmed my original suspicions.

I think that it (the use of the couch) really attacked me in the beginning. I used to make jokes with friends of mine about it. This was because I felt silly. Eventually I did forget and saw value in it; I find I talk differently. I go further without talking in a tangent. Without the usual face to face structure I have learned to talk more freely. Also I think it allows for more silence.

I don't like to lie on the couch. It makes you seem like an idiot in the light of these cartoons. It is like you are sick when you lie on the couch, like I was sick as a child . . . "Lie down; don't move!".

Most people on the couch in analysis cartoons are women. These cartoons really show hostility toward analysts. In these cartoons analysts just sit and grunt. There is hostility over the fact that no communication takes place. It often appears that the doctor doesn't really care whether the patient is there or not. Cartoons often show him asleep. The hostility is because the analyst doesn't talk; doesn't let anyone in on the problems.

I think the cartoons are caricatures. I see numerous things on television, movies, cartoons. It is distorted. It bears no relationship to what actually goes on. The analyst with a cigar or pipe leaning over the couch. But these things did influence me to fear the material aspects of therapy. These things are sadistic which created for me a forbidding conception of treatment. A frightening conception . . . The psychiatrist generally is portrayed as a sadistic cruel, deceitful, cold, aloof, snob of a person. A person who lives in another *über-mensch* world above everyone else.

Since psychiatry deals with absurdities, and absurdities are a prime basis for humor, you have these psychiatric jokes. Most people are really not directly in touch with psychiatry and would like to be. The cartoons make this possible and lets the one who can't go feel superior to those who can. Psychiatry is something on the mind of many people who are not in treatment. Most people are threatened and try to pass off through humor the threat they feel.

It hurts the way they mock psychiatry on television because I feel so vulnerable. I have a hard time separating my feelings from the things I learned in books in graduate school. I guess they enforce the idea you should be able to do it yourself, that makes it difficult to enter treatment. I saw a skit on television this past month and it really hurt—I guess because they don't talk freely about psychotherapy. Therapy is a strange, foul land they don't understand. These cartoons further picture the therapist as uninvolved, maladjusted, intellectualized idiots.

I feel ridiculous because the one unifying theme is this jerk lying on the couch and the other jerk is sitting there. It would embarrass me to see myself functioning in this way. The object of these cartoons is to make the psychiatrist look silly. And the patient is a fool to go to him and spend so much money.

Because the psychiatrist is supposed to know all about you; he has you all sized up. And people when they are afraid of something in themselves turn it into a joke. When people are afraid, jokes relieve them.

From the above we can observe that motivations explaining humor and the use of the couch in psychotherapy are many-sided. However, this humor, regardless of its source, serves as an inhibition to the therapeutic process for prospective patients considering treatment and those already committed to it. At some point in time, the patient is both subject and object. He is laughing at the cartoon or joke, and being laughed at through the process of identification with the characters.

We have shown how humor can channel and release much tension the public feels toward the process of psychoanalysis. A further examination reveals additional threats that psychoanalysis as symbolized by the couch can pose.

# Chapter 4

# THE COUCH AS A SYMBOL OF THE POSED THREATS OF PSYCHOANALYSIS

Two areas of great inhibition in society are human aggressive and sexual drives. There is talk of peace and yet perpetual war is waged. People sing and write poems of true love yet they dream of orgastic release and not love. Psychoanalysis has ruffled the waters of human denial of deeper passions and has forced them to admit the dichotomy between their feelings and their behavior. While critics of Freud often discount the treatment method he developed, they sometimes give recognition to many of his discoveries about the nature of humanity. George Miller (1969, p. 136), a past president of the American Psychological Association, dismissed psychoanalysis as a therapy of limited success. However, conceding a backhand compliment, he wrote:

> The impact of Freud's thought has been due far less to the instrumentalities he provided than to the changed conception of ourselves he inspired. Most important in the scale of

history has been his effect on the whole intellectual community and through them on the public at large. Today we are much more aware of the irrational components of man's nature and much better able to accept the reality of our unconscious impulses. The true importance of Freudian psychology derives far less from its scientific validity than from the effects that it has had on our shared image of man himself.

Miller's is a limited type of recognition. It is an acknowledgement of the threat to humanity's system of denial that psychoanalysis poses. Granted that such a threat exists, the threat is understandably circumscribed by a very strong system of defenses. The couch facilitates this system of defenses by existing as a symbol.

One such defense against the threat of psychoanalysis which is discussed in depth above, is ridicule of psychoanalysis through humor in which the couch plays a central role. The message can be translated: "It's not we who are crazy, it's these psychoanalysts who are crazy" (or who are sex maniacs or stupid). In many countries, such as those in the Iron Curtain, the practice of psychoanalysis is forbidden because psychoanalysis is treated on a par with any political or religious dogma that explains peoples' determinism as deriving from other than economic circumstances.

Another way of resisting its possible effectiveness is to insist that psychoanalysis lacks those elements which make a therapy scientific. The opponents of psychoanalysis imply that it has neither the means to evaluate an illness, nor the possibility of predicting outcome and thus does not have a verified potential for cure, or if it does, it is at best on a random basis.

A further method which quarantines psychoanalysis is to uphold the possibility that the theory may have some worth, but that the practice has little value. Dr. Miller does this when he refers to the limitation of Freud's "instrumentalities." A reference to the couch as psychoanalytic "in-

strumentality" brings to the surface the latent concern that
people harbor toward psychoanalysis.

A typical view of therapy is that the patient who is
engaging an analyst's services must willingly submit to him.
The person to whom he submits is deemed wise, independent, superior, and judgmental, while the patient feels ignorant, helpless, inferior, and contrite. Lying down is
traditionally associated with surrender and submission.
Since psychoanalytic patients do lie down, they are obvi-
ously susceptible to the inferior role that they envision
themselves playing during treatment. In direct contrast,
the analyst sits up, as though perched on a comfortable
throne.

This wide separation of roles runs counter to the
child's wish to remain infantile. Such a condition seemingly
imposed upon the patient appears in contradiction to the
patient/child's wish to reach out toward maturity. The analyst can appear as a villain and the couch as an instrument
of his slave trade. When the therapist is seen as a cold
unfriendly analyst or a quack, patients stiffen their bodies
against contact with his couch. Since our social habits discourage the outright expression of hostility toward a therapist, the release of the aggression is facilitated when it is
directed to the more easily attacked object, the couch,
when he is frustrated at the way the treatment is going, or
when he is angry at the analyst. He may refuse to lie on it
in periods of defiance toward the analyst/patient who sup-
posedly asks him to submit.

There can be great suspiciousness of the analyst's intentions. One sometimes hears stories of patients who are
changed for the worse as a result of psychoanalysis. The
couch may be approached with apprehension, as an element of such a change and possibly representing the unwanted outcome. If psychoanalysis is the catalyst that
uncovers guilt-laden sexual secrets or if it changes people
into sexually irresponsible individuals (and who knows by

what specific means this is accomplished?), the reclining position is an obvious danger to be avoided. The couch is a ready scapegoat for all this. It can come to stand for all the reprehensible sexuality and aggression that psychoanalysis is rumored to unleash upon its helpless victims.

Not all that the couch represents is bad. In addition to negative associations discussed above, the couch can also be a personal symbol of a benevolent process which is bringing the patient health, more emotional maturity and freedom and relief from former symptoms and fears. It can mean contact with the analyst as a kind, friendly, understanding human being. Since the couch belongs to the therapist, it is the closest the patients come to something of his.

## SYMBOLIC MEANINGS OF THE COUCH FOR THE ANALYST

The couch is also a symbol to the analyst. If he has ambivalent or negative feelings about his competence, the work he is doing, the kind of people he treats, or the isolation that the work enforces upon him, attitudes develop toward the couch which are manifestations of his doubts and resentments. Such conflicts may be expressed in his confusion as to when he should utilize it and his reasons for doing so.

In terms of counter-transference, the couch can be the bed of the analyst's fantasies. Like his patient, the analyst has thoughts, feelings, and fantasies. These elements of the analyst's mind are important aspects of the therapeutic process. For the analyst the couch as a symbol can be a stimulus for his never entirely resolved oedipal conflicts. The couch can be a means of giving expression to the voyeuristic opportunities that psychoanalysis as a process seems to offer him. If he has aspirations of superiority, the couch can be the valley of judgment on which he gazes from his lofty perch.

If psychoanalysis gratifies the therapist's needs to be part of an exclusive, highly intellectual club, his use of the couch may be for him the badge of his membership. Sherwood (1969) refers to psychoanalysis as having this intellectual distinction from other forms of psychotherapy. The couch, in this way, serves as a means of identification for the analyst.

Examining the meaning of the couch provides the psychoanalyst with an opportunity to continually study the process of his work with patients, and to examine how the process is regarded by society. Contrary to the expectations of its enemies and even the belief of some of its practitioners, psychoanalysis exists and grows in a cross current of popular opinion and social change. The public image, whether favorable or not, is a fact of life that we confront in treatment. If the number of psychoanalysts is few, their influence is disporportionately great. While the culture contains a great deal of "folk laughter," it also shows the enormous influence that psychoanalysis has upon our culture, its language, morals, philosophy, and science. In turn, the processes of psychoanalysis are influenced in many ways by public reaction to them.

All or some of this influence is represented in the patient's feelings about the treatment and its symbol, the couch. These considerations about the couch in terms of the patient's feelings and ideas may be an important part of the ultimate therapeutic alliance.

# Chapter 5

# THE HISTORY OF THE USE OF THE COUCH:

## *Developments in Psychoanalytic Theory and Practice*

The foundation and development of psychoanalysis, one of the monumental achievements in the history of psychiatry and indeed in the history of Western civilization, was essentially the work of a single man—Sigmund Freud. Early in his career he concluded that one must observe a phenomenon systemically in order to comprehend it. His insistence on this approach led to psychoanalysis being viewed as an acceptable method of scientific investigation. Because of this philosophy, Freud succeeded for the first time in explaining human behavior in clear terms and in demonstrating that under the proper circumstances, behavior can be changed.

Following his leadership, psychoanalysts established that the study of personality could have the same operational and cumulative characteristics as the natural sciences.

Freud began his work in an era dominated by the natural sciences. He was able to succeed where other attempts to introduce psychological approaches into psychiatry and medicine had consistently failed. He was able to succeed because he demonstrated the principle of psychological causality. He introduced specific methods of observation into the field of personality research and was able to apply a technique of clinical inquiry that was compatible with the nature of the phenomenon that was to be investigated. Instead of formulating general philosophical speculations about the nature of the human personality, Freud studied intensively the behavior of individuals (The Wolf-Man, 1971). Later the myriad patterns formed by people in the larger social fabric of mankind were also studied (Freud, 1912b, 1927a, 1930).

In his efforts to probe and enlarge the understanding of human nature, Freud had very little assistance other than an unusually fertile and perceptive mind and a dedication to the principles of scientific truth. In the face of considerable frustration and professional isolation during his beginning years, he persisted in an attempt to understand the often seemingly inconsistent and contradictory thinking and behavior patterns of his patients. Gradually he developed verbal methods and techniques which elucidated mental conditions that were previously considered a matter of speculation. Freud had no tools or instruments to assist him in his efforts except one: the couch. We are fortunate that this artifact, unlike many of mankind's significant relics, has a well documented and complete history readily available. Freud's couch, the first used in psychoanalysis, has been photographed many times and remains today in London, an object of persistent curiosity.

## PSYCHOANALYTIC DIALECTICS: HISTORICAL EARLY ROOTS OF THE COUCH

Although popular belief holds that Freud was the first therapist to use the couch for psychoanalysis, Halpern (1963, p. 419) claimed differently:

The first recorded psychoanalytic treatment took place not in a heavily furnished Viennese consulting room in the Bergasse, but at the Dionysium, an open-air theater nestled against the southeast slope of the Athenian Acropolis. On the couch in place of the aristocractic Elizabeth Von Ritter reclined the rustic figure of an Attic farmer, Strepsiades; behind the patient, not the bearded immaculate Herr Dr. Professor Sigmund Freud, but dirty-foot, satyr-faced Socrates.

*Socrates:* Come, lie down here.
*Strepsiades:* What for?
*Socrates:* Ponder awhile over matters that interest you.
*Strepsiades:* Oh, I pray not there.
*Socrates:* Come, on the couch:
*Strepsiades:* What a cruel fate.
*Socrates:* Ponder and examine closely, gather your thoughts together, let your mind turn to every side of things. If you meet with difficulty, spring quickly to some other idea: keep away from sleep.

The "analysis" goes on until Strepsiades, under Socrates' urgings and interpretations, eventually thinks of controlling the waxing and waning of the moon so that the months will cease and his monthly bills never come due. (Alexander and Selesnick, 1966, p. xiii)

This scene, which first made Athenians laugh about 433 B.C., forces us today to compare the action on stage to the familiar image of a contemporary psychoanalyst treating his patient. In his play *The Clouds,* Aristophanes portrays Socrates as a healer who treats on a couch the Greek farmer Strepsiades. Though this portrayal lacked the elements of a purposeful study of resistance and transference (and therefore hardly a process that could be termed pysychoanalysis) this, nevertheless, may be the first written mention of a couch being used for therapeutic purposes.

Why did Socrates put Strepsiades on the couch? For those seeking help from a healer/physician, the use of the recumbent position has been taken for granted throughout history as a possible aspect of the examination or treatment (Alexander and Selesnick, 1966). Since, traditionally, very sick people are bedridden, it has been expected that they be reclining while the healer sits up. (Hence, the well-known phrase "bedside manner" in referring to the physician's administering to his patient.)

Socrates wished to induce relaxation, a wish which usually finds its greatest fulfillment in the supine position. Most people lie down when they want to nap. (Socrates was aware of the possibility that Strepsiades might fall asleep, so he warned his patient to stay awake.) In this position the possibilities of relinquishing certain attachments to regular alert patterns of everyday life are enhanced. Although Aristophanes was not aware that this relinquishing of wakeful patterns also introduces the opportunity for new thoughts and feelings to come to consciousness. Freud many centuries later would investigate this phenomenon.

For someone suffering from psychic stress the remedy often is to induce calmness. A natural means for developing relaxation is through one of the most ancient approaches, hypnosis, often in conjunction with the use of the reclining position. To utilize hypnosis, which was Freud's first approach to the treatment of hysteria, he and other hypnotists encouraged the use of the recumbent position (Alexander & Selesnick, 1966). For one thing, hypnosis was considered an approximation of sleep. For another, the physician had to hover nearby in order to direct the procedure, and often it was most comfortable in long sessions for the patient to be reclining and have the doctor sit close to him.

A number of well-known French doctors, Charcot, Bernheim, and Liebout, found that they could successfully treat large numbers of neurotic patients with the use of hypnotherapy. Freud's (1892a) introduction to the practice of hypnosis was through Charcot with whom he studied. The first principal method of therapy he applied to neurotic patients was an outgrowth of his work with Charcot at Salpetriere Hospital in France. After studying with Charcot for a year, he later visited hypnotists Bernheim and Liebout to observe their work. When eventually Freud returned from France to practice in Vienna, he developed a close association with Josef Breuer who was also utilizing hypnosis successfully to treat neurotic patients. One of the most famous and successful treatments of neurosis, the case of Anna O., was treated by Breuer with hypnosis. (Breur and Freud, 1895) She is credited with having coined the term, "the talking cure," which is now applied to psychoanalysis.

Deeply impressed with what he observed in France and with the results that Breuer obtained, Freud eagerly employed these methods with his own patients. He used the couch to help relax his "neurotic" patients and to encourage them to regress and recall their early memories. For his patients, the couch seemed not only to facilitate relaxation, but also to make the sessions more comfortable. While they reclined, Freud too could relax more comfortably, as compared to facing them with the increased demands for attention the upright position required. However, from the very beginning of his practice of neurology, Freud as a practicing hypnotist and physician met with considerable trouble and opposition in Vienna. After returning from his studies with Charcot in France, his attempts to introduce newly-acquired French notions concerning hysteria and hypnosis were greeted with scorn by professional colleagues, since the prevailing view at that time was that neurosis was an organic disorder of the brain. Freud was soon excluded from almost all academic life and from attendance at medical societies.

Undaunted, Freud remained loyal to his teacher, Charcot, despite this great opposition and continued to hold him in especially high esteem. He said (1893, pp. 22–23):

> Charcot's application of the phenomena of hypnosis to hysteria enabled a very great advance to be made in this impor-

tant sphere of hitherto and despised facts, because the weight of his reputation put an end once and for all to doubts of the reality of hypnotic manifestations.

As far as Freud's early practice was concerned, his "therapeutic arsenal contained only two weapons," he said (1925, p. 26), "electrotherapy and hypnotism, for prescribing a visit to a hydropathic establishment after a single consultation was an inadequate source of income."

This left hypnotism which, as mentioned earlier, was branded by the Viennese psychiatric brotherhood as not only fraudulent, but dangerous. Despite the increasing recognition accorded Charcot, hypnotists were nevertheless regarded as individuals operating beyond the scope of medicine and were treated with cold scientific contempt and distance. From 1886, when Freud returned from Charcot's clinic until he developed the "free association" method (sometime between 1892 and 1895), hypnosis was the principle method of therapy Freud (1889, 1891, 1892b, 1901) utilized to understand and treat his patients.

Along with Josef Breuer, much of Freud's work involved visiting bedridden patients in their homes. Later, Breuer was given special acknowledgement by Freud for his part in the development of psychoanalysis, an outgrowth of the hypnotic/cathartic method. Freud credited Breuer with the discovery of this method. He said (1905, pp. 259–260):

> There are many ways and means of practicing psychotherapy. All that lead to recovery are good . . . We have developed the technique of hypnotic suggestion, and psychotherapy by diversion of attention, by exercise, and by eliciting suitable affects. I despise none of these methods and would use all of them under proper conditions. If I have come to confine myself to one form of treatment, to the method that Breuer called "catharsis" which I myself prefer to call "analytic," it is because I have allowed myself to be influenced by purely subjective motives. Because of the part

I have played in founding this therapy, I feel a personal
obligation to devote myself to closer investigation of it and
to the development of its technique.

In his preface to Bernheim's book *Hypnotism and Suggestion,* Freud (1888) attempted to surmount the objections of
the public and of the medical profession to the use of hypnotism as therapeutic method. In review, Freud's arguments still remain interesting, with the objections he
outlined not limited to hypnosis, for they come to be repeated many times with reference to psychoanalysis. The
readers were assured by Freud that the hypnotist did not
put ideas into his patient's mind, nor did he create the
symptoms. Just as the then prevalent fear of being harmed
by anesthesia was unfounded, so too Freud said was the
fear of being harmed by hypnosis. He argued both hypnotism and anesthesia were comparable to natural sleep, and
just as a resistance to chloroform was overcome by familiarity and reason, so too might the resistance to being hypnotized be overcome.

In defending hypnotic sleep the same reasons and arguments were used by Freud as were by early anesthetists.
Both anesthetists and hypnotists relieved the anxieties of
hesitant patients and members of the medical profession by
inviting a comparison between their methods and natural
sleep. Although they are heirs to Freud's early use of hypnotism, psychoanalysts no longer consider their method
related to sleep. Despite this, the resistances expressed by
those who were opposed to anesthesia and hypnosis are
also often heard in regard to psychoanalysis. Patients
feared what they might say if they were relaxed by hypnosis
or by anesthetics, and what they might do if they abandoned voluntary control. Therefore, in considering the resistances to treatment, we find thrown together those
resistances to anesthesia, hypnosis, and psychoanalysis. In
this sense the recumbent position is a relic. To analytic

historians, it is a reminder that psychoanalysis had its origin in hypnotism. The surprising fact remains that even though he eventually abandoned hypnosis, Freud continued to utilize the recumbent position.

## FREUD'S TRANSITION TO PSYCHOANALYSIS

Although Freud found his hypnotic treatment of neurotic patients reasonably successful, there were, nevertheless, a number of difficulties with this method. It was hard work and a large number of patients could not be consistently hypnotized. Of those patients who could be consistently hypnotized, there was often a recurrence of symptoms in patients for whom the results initially seemed positive. He said (1905, p. 261):

> I gave up the suggestion technique, and with it hypnosis, so early in my practice because I despaired of making suggestion powerful and enduring enough to effect permanent cures. In all severe cases I saw suggestions which had been applied crumble away again; and then the disease or some substitute for it returned.

His work in psychoanalysis was an outgrowth of hypnotic technique. He said (1925, p. 49):

> This seemed a more laborious process than putting them into hypnosis, but it might prove highly instructive. So I abandoned hypnotism, only retaining my practice of requiring the patient to lie upon a sofa while I sat behind him, seeing him, but not seen myself.

Freud (1905a, p. 261) further stated:

> Besides all this I have another reproach against this method (hypnosis) namely, that it conceals from us all insight into the play of mental forces; it does not permit us, for example, to recognize the resistance with which the patient clings to

his disease and thus even fights against his own recovery; yet it is this phenomenon of resistance which alone makes it possible to comprehend this behavior in daily life.

With his increased understanding of unconscious mental processes, an alternative method of uncovering patient's conflicts was discovered. Suggestion technique and hypnosis were given up by Freud in favor of another technique, that of free association, which he found to have applicability to a larger number of patients and which seemed to have more lasting results. Thompson (1950, pp. 82–83) said: "Thus free association was discovered and it was soon apparent that it has an advantage over hypnosis in that the patient remained conscious and did not have to be informed later of what had taken place." Speaking of the shift from hypnosis to free-association Roazen (1975, p. 82) says: "The couch was a useful remnant from Freud's use of hypnosis, however, since it permitted both analyst and patient to relax and free-associate without the burden (at least to Freud) of direct face-to-face confrontations".

Free association was Freud's first contribution to the technique and was unique in many ways. This technique not only required cooperation on the part of the patient, but it also required considerable verbal activity of a nonjudgmental and nondirected kind absent from customary verbal communication. Coltrera and Ross (1967, p. 19) in their article, "Freud's Psychoanalytic Technique—From the Beginnings to 1923" go into considerable detail in describing this unique development:

> The shift from deliberate suggestion and concentration to free association represents more than a simple progression in technique. For the device of free association facilitates the thinning out of the quantitative and qualitative distributions of attention cathexes necessary for the "widening of attention" previously effected by hypnotic suggestion and the technique of concentration in the cathartic method. There-

fore, the "basic rule" of free association is implemented by the stimulus—deprived situation of the nonintrusive analyst, the use of the couch and the radical restriction of reality cues, each of which is directed to the end of inducing a topographic regression, represented phenomenologically as a "widening of attention." For, with the "widening of attention," the ever topographic regressive direction of the states of consciousness of the analytic situation—and its correlate, topographically regressed states of reflective awarenesses—facilitates the appearance of the least-hypercathected unconscious derivative able to escape the work of repression in the preconscious.

In free associating, the patient was asked to speak in as continuous a fashion as possible during the periods of treatment describing, without reservation, whatever thoughts, feelings, and memories came to mind. Because relaxation and the absence of outside stimulation seemed to facilitate this process, Freud continued encouraging his patients to lie on the couch facing away from him, as he had them do when he practiced suggestion and hypnosis.

Gedo and Pollock (1967, pp. 564–565) in exploring the origins of the use of the couch state the following:

> The use of the couch was originally necessitated by the requirement of applying hand pressure to the patient's head in the effort to overcome the resistance against recollection. This technique was utilized for a number of years after the abandonment of hypnosis. The analyst is still sitting (more or less) within arm's length of the patient's head. After Freud had abandoned the laying-on of hands (having found interpretation of resistance an easier and less demanding method of overcoming it than hectoring the patient had been), he continued to sit out of the patient's sight. Freud once expressed personal distaste for being looked at throughout the days as one reason for this choice, an explanation that Jones, for one, has found unconvincing.

Roazen (1975, p. 123) believes the question of being looked at was a basic factor in Freud's use of the couch and by identification with Freud, his followers were also sensitive to being looked at. He says:

> Unlike some therapists, Freud chose to rely on the analytic couch so that he would not have to be watched, all day; as he explained it,
>
>> I cannot put up with being stared at by other people for eight hours a day (or more). Since, while I am listening to the patient, I, too give myself over to the current of my unconscious thoughts, I do not wish my expressions of face to give the patient material for interpretations or to influence him in what he tells me. The patient usually regards being made to adopt this position as a hardship and rebels against it. . . .
>
> Rituals can serve a positive function, and Freud considered the use of a couch as "ceremonial." [Freud, 1913b] But the use of the couch became the touchstone of analysis, and analysts feared that if they did not use a couch they would not be proper analysts.

The so-called Wolf-Man, one of Freud's earliest patients, offered an additional motive for Freud's use of the couch. The Wolf-Man (1971, p. 142) writes:

> During a psychoanalytic treatment of long duration the patient often has the opportunity of discussing all manner of things with the physician. Freud told me once, for example, how the "psychoanalytic situation" came about. This "situation," as is well known, is that of the patient lying on the couch with the analyst sitting near the couch in a position where he cannot be seen by the analysand. Freud told me that he had originally sat at the opposite end of the couch, so that analyst and analysand could look at each other. One female patient, exploiting this situation, made all possible—or rather impossible—attempts to seduce him. To rule out anything similar, once and for all, Freud moved from his earlier position to the opposite end of the couch.

What was unique about the use of the couch by Freud was that by consistently using the couch, it became identified with him and with psychoanalysis. It should be mentioned however, that Freud did not use only the recumbent position in treating patients. He is known to have treated them sitting up on occasion and even taking walks with them as in the case of Gustave Mahler (Jones, 1955).

## POST-FREUD DEVELOPMENTS

Many of Freud's early adherents, who later departed from his theoretical views continued to utilize the couch, either consistently, or with certain patients and some modifications. Among these were Wilhelm, Stekel, Carl Jung, Wilhelm Reich, Otto Rank, and Karen Horney. The fact that they departed from many of the tenets of classic psychoanalysis, but retained the use of the couch may have some general implications for the relationship between a theory of psychotherapy and the use of the couch. It might suggest that the use of the recumbent position has an inherent value useful in many types of psychotherapies. Some therapists, in contrast, seem to have abandoned the use of the couch. Among them were Alfred Adler, Harry Stack Sullivan, Erich Fromm, Frieda Fromm-Reichmann, and Clara Thompson. For the most part, however, the use of the couch has persisted and even increased. This increase was mainly due to the development and spread of psychoanalytic training institutes.

For all analytic students, the couch is probably the first encounter they have with the technique of psychoanalysis. Before knowing much about psychoanalysis or about psychoanalytic procedure, they know of the use of the couch because it is part of their own analysis. The students later learn in the course of their academic training that the use of the couch is taken for granted as an essential part of treatment. The student analyst through identification with his own analyst, through his acquired comfort with the analytic process, and as a result of his own studies, will likely continue the use of the couch with his patients. Because identification is one of the earliest and strongest learning mechanisms, it often persists in the face of reason and even opposition. This may help explain why the use of the couch is carried on without too much examination of the process. The student who later himself becomes an analyst has strong ties of identification with his own analyst/teacher. Thus, it is that he follows in the tradition of his analyst and teachers.

In terms of training, Freud never attended a psychoanalytic institute, and never had an analytic supervisor. Neither did he ever give anyone a "training analysis," or teach courses in a psychoanalytic institute, nor did he undertake explicity to supervise anyone's psychoanalytic cases. Freud's training beyond medical school was as a physiologist and as a neurologist, both areas being considerably removed from the verbal and symbolic work of psychoanalysis. Therefore, for him psychiatric training could not be an aspect of his psychoanalytic work. His approach to doing psychoanalytic work was not doctrinaire, but rather quite pragmatic. He had no one to teach him to use or not to use the couch in his psychoanalytic work. Its employment arose from its usefulness and benefit to the kind of therapy he was doing and the results he was attempting to attain. In this respect, while his early followers emulated his efforts they nevertheless made distinguished contributions of their own. Freud's early students Wilhelm Stekel, Alfred Adler, Sandor Ferençzi and others often had long walks and long talks with him. He communicated to them what he was doing and provided them with suggestions as to technique and ideas about the patients that they were endeavoring to treat by this new approach. It is meaningful that the early psychoanalysts, those practicing before about 1922, were without the benefit of any formal training in psychoanalysis. Until the first training institute was established, a student of psychoanalysis could only learn from a senior analyst, i.e., the oral tradition via the preceptorship system.

In Roazen's (1975, p. 118) opinion the way that Freud related to his pupils was such that, until the numbers grew beyond his capacity to teach, he could quite adequately teach without formalizing technique. He says:

> One of the reasons for Freud's influence is that his therapeutic procedure was much more disciplined and orderly than anything anybody else has been able to devise. Freud remained highly rationalistic when it came to technique. He had been reluctant to write about his special approach until his quarrels with Adler, Stekel, and Jung, when it seemed advisable to distinquish his own form of treatment from that of other psychotherapists. Freud was too wise to be dogmatic about technique, and above all he wanted his pupils to be good understanders; perhaps he wrote so little on technique in order not to lay down the law too restrictively for his followers.

It was not until almost 30 years after Freud began practicing psychoanalysis that the first psychoanalytic institute was formed in Berlin under the direction of Karl Abraham. With the establishment of this institute new concepts were formulated as to which techniques that would best implement psychoanalytic treatment should be taught to analytic students. Also established were training procedures such as required analysis for all candidates, prescribed courses, and analysis of patients under supervision until the student was considered competent to practice on his own. It is likely that the use of the couch was also institutionalized by this formalization of psychoanalytic training. Freud never played an active part in this formalization. Possibly it was his own difficult beginnings that made him hesitate to embrace any tradition.

Even with the early abandonment of hypnosis, Freud's

popularity did not increase in Vienna, nor did his loyalty and respect for his medical colleagues in that ancient city return. In many ways Freud moved away from medicine. It could be said that the only material vestige of his former medical activities was the couch. All other instruments and drugs were abandoned. As psychoanalysis became more widespread and well known, many people came to him to learn about it. Freud welcomed those from many avenues of interest to his fold: lawyers (Hans Sachs), psychologists (Theodore Reik), theologists (Oscar Pfister), art curators (Ernst Kris) as well as many physicians—many of whom were not trained as psychiatrists. It is well known that Freud discouraged many people from proceeding with medical training including his own daughter Anna.

Because the couch is linked to psychoanalysis, and in many people's minds psychoanalysis is considered a medical treatment, Freud's personal orientation toward medicine is a matter of some interest. He (1927b, pp. 252–253) had some memorable things to say in this area:

> Psychoanalysis falls under the heading of psychology; not of medical psychology in the old sense, nor of the psychology of morbid processes, but simply of psychology. . . . The possibility of its application to medical purposes must not lead us astray. . . . It is argued that psychoanalysis was after all discovered by a physician in the course of his efforts to assist his patients. But, that is clearly neither here nor there.

> I should like to consider the historical argument a moment longer. Since it is with me personally that we are concerned, I can throw a little light, for anyone who may be interested, on my own motives. After forty-one years of medical activity, my self-knowledge tells me that I have never really been a doctor in the proper sense. I became a doctor through being compelled to deviate from my original purpose; and the triumph of my life lies in my having, after a long and round-about journey, found my way back to my earliest path.

But while Freud successfully avoided engaging himself in the institutionalization of psychoanalysis, the mainstream of the development of the profession proceeded through the various schools that were gradually established all over the world. Millett (1962, p. 128) describes this process of the institutionalization of psychoanalysis as taking on the character of ritual. He asserts that the very use of a procedure by Freud was itself a basis for blind imitation. He says:

> What began as a specialized mode of inquiry and treatment led to the formation of special laws or regulations which began to take on the character of ritual. The couch, free association, strict attendance, the relation and interpretation of dreams, high frequency of sessions, prompt payment of fees—all such requirements came to be accepted as the *sine qua non* of psychoanalytic practice. Authority for this rigid procedural framework was derived from the usage by the Master, and was slavishly reproduced by his disciples as they spread the new gospel among their successors. Thus was firmly established the highly authoritarian system of psychoanalytic organization and practice which provided the model for the introduction of this new method of study and treatment to the world.

Lorand (1950, p. 208) has also mentioned the effect of the institution upon the analyst in training:

> In the course of many years of analytic work, I have had the opportunity to observe, in working with younger colleagues who are in the process of being trained, the influence upon them of the changes of training programs, expansion of subjects and also the shifting of their theoretical orientations. With students or patients who have transferred from another colleague, one often meets with ideas which differ from one's own and from those generally accepted. Sometimes an analyst favors a particular theoretical point of view and repeatedly refers to it. An analyst may be led on by scientific interest to prove the validity of a concept to which he feels a predilection . In some cases it can be an emotional

attitude based on "training transference" which causes an
analyst to overemphasize one viewpoint.

Because of a generation gap between those analysts
who were trained, if one can call it that, under the loose
aegis of Freud, and those who began to emerge during the
1920s as graduates of psychoanalytic institutes, much of
what analysts later learned was communicated in what is
called the "oral tradition," that which is talked about, possibly taken for granted, and seldom put into print.

Moser (1977) (p. 29) also shows how the influence of
one's analyst can activate a student's behavior:

> . . . it is as if he were sitting behind me, my guardian angel,
> in those analysis and therapies I am now conducting myself.

It may be that the oral tradition, i.e., unwritten guidelines, in psychoanalysis has some analogy to the role that
writing played in the history of mankind. Before he learned
to write, man passed on, in the "oral tradition," knowledge
from father to son and around the tribal campfire elders to
younger tribesmen. Writing for mankind began only about
5,000 years ago. Formal training for psychoanalysts began
only about 50 years ago. Vestiges of the "oral tradition" in
psychoanalysis as they apply to the use of the couch may
help explain why heretofore so little has been written about
it. It is conceivable that the use of the couch in psycholanal-
ysis is at a point of development where more written recognition of its role in theory and technique is now possible.

# Chapter 6

# THE THEORY OF REPRESSION AS APPLIED TO THE COUCH

Psychoanalysts consider their profession to be a scientific one for good reason. They consider that psychoanalysis operates according to scientific theory and method. The principles and theories of this science are asserted to be logical and rational; it is only the subject matter which is illogical and irrational (Fenichel, 1945).

Freud developed in almost 20 years, a relatively short peric of time, a comprehensive conceptualization of the human mind. While much of this structure seems to rest upon proven facts, other areas have yet to be validated. Throughout his lifetime Freud continued to update and revise his theories, and since his death in September, 1939 others have continued this process of revision. Principal among these have been Anna Freud, Heinz Hartmann, Ernest Kris, Rudolph Lowenstein, Jacob Arlow, and Charles Brenner.

Roazen (1975, p. 164) speaks of Freud's practice of revising his theoretical formulations as follows:

Freud's urge to structure clinical material into formulas was of a piece with his therapeutic aim of leading the patient away from primitive emotional reactions. He was more interested in the magic of words than of gestures, and he relied on the patient's ability to verbalize his problems. The use of the couch forced the analyst to rely all the more on the rationalistic power of verbal insight.

We can see here another observation of Freud's continual strivings to rework his theories and techniques not only to better explain the facts of mental life, but also to guide the therapy toward becoming a more progressive instrument of positive mental change. Roazen supports here Freud's use of the couch as a facilitator of this change.

The principles of psychoanalytic theory, which were mainly conceived by Freud, were developed out of the challenge to explain certain operations of the human mind that were not well understood previously. Starting with broad and sometimes rough hypotheses, he gradually forged the observations he had accumulated into the exact principles that now constitute psychoanalytic theory. But what Freud developed was more than a theory. It was a technique for investigating mental processes that outlined clinical procedure and the therapeutic process (Gedo & Pollock, 1976).

A theory must account for the observable facts in order to be considered valid. For psychoanalytic technique to be valid, it must confirm the theory (Waelder, 1964). Understanding the theory should lead to the development of correct technique, which in turn, should result in forms of treatment that bring about increasingly greater predictability of outcome. Therefore, for the analyst, the study of theory is a never-ceasing search for more data and ideas to enlarge the scope of his understanding. Thus, one of Freud's first theories postulated the existence of the "unconscious" (1915). He explained that in neurosis ideas were repressed and cathected by the unconscious part of the mind so that they strove to become conscious, but failed to do so, due to the countercathexis of the conscious part of the mind. This concept of the mind was topographical in the sense that it assumed different levels: conscious, preconscious, and unconscious; this model was further economic in the sense that varying quantities of cathexis could be invested in or against a repressed idea; and there was a dynamic aspect in the sense that an idea could move through the various levels of the mind.

From this initial structural theory Freud developed a technique to treat patients having a psychoneurosis. His use of hypnosis was an attempt to raise unconscious mind functions to the conscious level, but he later shifted to the use of free association. While he found that free association led to the revelation of basic unconscious conflicts, he found that certain mental processes in his patients appeared to oppose his efforts to make what was repressed conscious. He then developed what were to become two basic formulations of psychoanalysis: the theories of "resistance" and "transference."

Jones (1953, p. 284) describes the origin of Freud's theories of resistance and transference as follows:

> His own observations of the phenomena of "resistance" and "transference" date from about 1890 and 1892 respectively. In later years he declared these two concepts to be the hallmark of psychoanalysis. Freud's most important and original contribution in this field was his discovery (1894) that psychoneuroses are due to an intolerance of memories concerning sexual experiences in childhood; this led later to the recognition of childhood sexuality (1898).

Freud found that with the use of free association he could better reveal, identify, study, and resolve these resistances that prevented the repressed ideas from becoming conscious. Freud learned that when he could resolve his patients' resistances, repressed ideas could come to consciousness and be discussed, and those conflicts in which the neurosis had been embedded could be resolved.

## THE COUCH AS AN AID TO REGRESSION

In his work of attempting to bring repressed feelings, thoughts, and experiences to consciousness, Freud found a puzzling phenomenon operating. In the course of treatment most of his patients' perceptions of him changed so that for each of them he was cast in a role of someone from their remote past. While at first this misperception was considered a disagreeable barrier in the treatment situation, Freud soon found an explanation for this phenomenon, developed a theory to explain it, and turned this cognitive distortion in the relationship into a therapeutic advantage. This theory explained the distortion in the therapeutic relationship Freud called transference. The theory included the concept of regression and repression. Jones (1953, p. 285) says of this development:

> In 1892 he was writing about the tendency of the mind to produce "antithetical ideas" that interfered with conscious intentions. But before this he had sensed the effort needed to overcome opposition in his patients' minds to recovering the forgotten memories, opposition to which he gave the name "resistance." He then easily inferred that the resistance keeping the memories from consciousness was simply another name for the force that had pushed them away to start with, one for which he first termed "defense" and before long "repression."

Repression played an important role in the psychoanalytic treatment of neurosis in that the mind eliminated from consciousness the memory of the original conflict, but in a sense retained it by enacting with an analyst years later the main elements of the conflict in terms of feelings and distorted perceptions. This distortion of time, place, and person is the phenomenon of transference. Transference operates through the mechanism of displacement (treating one or more persons or things as another) and regression (treating the present as though it were the past).

Freud (1917a) identified two forms of regression, that in which the libido returned to the original object, which explained the phenomenon of transference, and that in which the libido returned to the infantile sexual organization stage, such as the oral or anal phase of development.

Freud enlarged still further the theoretical scope of psychoanalytic understanding when he amplified the topographical view of the mind with the organizations ego, superego, and id. Other writers continued this work (Anna Freud, 1946b).

Regression was seen as a defense of the ego and also as a function of the ego. All ego functions could undergo regression. When a tired child stopped walking and demanded to be carried regression in terms of motility was observed. Suggesting a patient abandon all movement and lie on the couch may also be promoting regression of motility. Sleep, dreams, fantasies, or daydreams are forms of regression that occur naturally. Sensory deprivation (which can be experimentally controlled) can induce regression in the perceptual systems.

Regression is usually assumed present in states of anxiety and also can be a source of anxiety in that it signals the presence of some kind of threat to the ego. Shur (1958, pp. 194–95) has written:

> (There is) the assumption that in neurotic anxiety we are dealing with a temporary, partial ego regression. This regression always involves: a. the function of the ego which designates a situation as dangerous, i.e., evaluation of dan-

ger. It may also involve: b. the type of reaction to this evaluation. Ego regression tends toward early fixations as does id regression, with the points of fixations depending on genetic and environmental factors. I have also suggested the prevalence of primary processes is one of the main elements in anxiety.

With neurotic conflict we usually observe some form of anxiety. This anxiety according to Shur, in itself has a tendency toward regression. This regression mobilizes and reveals the points of fixation and the primary process thinking that in analysis forms a blueprint for therapeutic reconstruction.

Under certain conditions some authors view regression as a normal process (Alexander, 1956; Arlow, 1960; Kris, 1952). For example, during puberty regression is observed as a common phenomenon and is probably necessary to allow the kind of psychic reorganization that is characteristic of that period. Object loss in death causes regression and aids in the mourning process that permits the emotional reorganization needed for new object relationships. It can be observed that functions may be assisted by regression. The main characteristics of these regressions in the service of the ego is that they are controlled (Kris, 1952). "That is, a partial and fluctuating relaxation of ego controls and orientation to allow normally preconscious or unconscious material some access to consciousness in the interest of performing a certain creative task" (Schafer, 1954, p. 215). These regressions are temporary, circumscribed, and they are reversible. In controlled regression ego function is not overwhelmed, and the ego maintains control over id such as fantasy. Under these conditions the derivatives are available to consciousness. This type of regression assists creative thinking, intuition, and imagination. Enhanced communication develops between the ego and the id and the mobile cathexis of the primary process is available for secondary process utilization.

Bion (1958, p. 349) has given us a dramatic example of such controlled regression:

> The patient has arrived on time and I have asked for him to be called. As he passes into the room he glances rapidly at me; such frank scrutiny has been a development of the past six months and is still a novelty.
>
> While I close the door he goes to the foot of the couch, facing the head pillows and my chair, and he stands, shoulders stooping, knees sagging, head inclined to the chair, motionless until I have passed him and am about to sit down. So closely do his movements seem to be geared with mine that the inception of my movement to sit appears to release a spring in him. As I lower myself into my seat he turns about, slowly, evenly, as if something would be spilled, or perhaps fractured, were he to be betrayed into a precipitate movement. As I sit, the turning movement stops as if we were both parts of the same clockwork toy.

Bion (p. 342) explains the meaning of this behavior:

> When the patient glanced at me he was taking a part of me into him. It was taken into his eyes, as I later interpreted this thought to him, as if his eyes could suck something out of me. This was then removed from me, before I sat down, and expelled, again through his eyes, so that it was deposited in the right-hand corner of the room where he could keep it under observation while he was lying on the couch.

The threat of losing sight of his analyst, to Bion's patient, was so severe that he defended himself against this by introjecting and then projecting Bion. This aspect of the regressive features of the couch has been referred to earlier.

To adequately consider the use of the couch in relation to the analytic theory of regression requires some formulation of the significance of the patient's and analyst's physical positioning, and its relationship to the emotional and ideational responses that may or may not arise as a result of this positioning. The concept of the couch as a causal factor of regression is a consideration here. Another is the concept of external vs. internal stimulation and their differing effects on the mental processes.

In denying the patient the opportunity of seeing the analyst, leaving him with only an inanimate room as sensory stimulus, a condition of mild sensory deprivation is subtly created. It is well known that when deprived of external stimuli, the perceptual appartus of the mental system withdraws its attention from the external world and looks within.

In a classical laboratory experiment with sensory deprivation, stimuli impinging on the subject's senses can be modified so that as few cues as possible can be picked up from the external environment. Laboratory experiments have repeatedly demonstrated that many subjects experiencing auditory and perceptual sensory deprivation begin to perceive internal stimuli very intensely and/or to hallucinate (Zuckerman, *et al.,* 1968).

Granting that such perceptions are an aspect of sensory deprivation, it is understandable that the analytic situation can precipitate some of these symptoms in the patient. The passivity on the couch, the exclusion of sounds —except for the patient's own voice and, less frequently, the analyst's—and the lack of any variable visual stimuli presumably serve to heighten the perception of internal awareness of thoughts and feelings. This may account for some of the hypnogogic experiences this author has heard my patients on the couch describe, such as: "I just saw a man running without a head," and, "I hear the sound of a waterfall," or, "For a moment I was seeing bright flashes of color."

In a study of the role of the recumbent position, Zubek and MacNeill (1967, p. 148) found that many dramatic subjective experiences result solely from perceptual isolation. Among these may be the transient loss of contact with reality, speech difficulties, changes in body image, and hallucinatory-like expressions. It was found that "both the isolated and recumbent control subjects experienced a greater incidence of complex and vivid dreams, worry and fright, hunger and restlessness than did the ambulatory controls."

The results of this study indicate that most of the "dramatic" subjective phenomena, previously reported in the isolation literature, resulted solely from perceptual isolation. Among these are hallucinatory-like experiences, temporal disorientation, and speech difficulties. Other symptoms such as boredom, religious preoccupation, and changes in self-appraisal appear to be due to the combined effects of perceptual isolation and recumbency.

According to Kris (1951), the recumbent position tends to increase the number of projections and diminish the amount of objective perceptions. Deprived of animate stimuli that an actual view of the analyst affords him, the patient creates or projects the reaction he imagines that the analyst has toward him. It would follow from this that past reactions and present projections would come more readily into prominence in this posture. Transference phenomena so essential to the success of the analysis is thus further facilitated. This is done by a principle of mental functioning which explains why there is a tendency to project past experiences onto a present situation in possibly a distorted way when actual information is not available.

Haak (1957, p. 186) insists that the regressive factor is the most important aspect of the use of the couch:

> Lying down implies, on the one hand, being a child, on the other being sick, helpless, defenseless, female, passive. Furthermore, the most important means of contact with the outer world, namely the visual object-relation, is broken off as the analyst sits behind the patient. The contact is exclusively maintained through hearing, and this stimulates infantile fantasies.

Haak in his observations confirms that the recumbent position before it is even assumed by the patient symbolizes not only a regressive, but a negative posture and one that would arouse anxiety at its suggestion. He further observes that eye contact is reality contact and that the lack of visual stimulation leads to an internal or narcissistic object state. Hearing which is then the remaining reality contact provides an easier path to regressive fantasy. Spitz (1956) also emphasizes the fact that the patient is lying down and therefore is lower than the analyst who is sitting upright behind him, that the patient's bodily movements and locomotion are limited, and that he cannot see the person to whom he speaks; all of which push the patient in the direction of being objectless. In a sense this condition resembles the prattling of a child in that we ask him to say everything without discrimination and without responsibility.

Further illustrating the regressive factor in the use of the recumbent position, Shields (1964) discusses the case of one of his patients, who was incapable of staying on the couch for more than a few minutes at a time because lying on the couch meant that the analyst might have ceased to exist or might have been absorbed by the patient. The patient also feared that she would sink into the couch and disappear. Khan (1962) also emphasizes that the routine of having a patient lie on the couch contributes to regression in a variety of ways.

Greenacre (1954) suggests that the circumstance in which two people meet together repeatedly over a long period of time makes for an intensity of emotional involvement. The fact that one is troubled and relatively helpless and the other expert and offering help, facilitates an uneven, "tilted" relationship, with the troubled one tending to regress to some form of infantile dependency. She contends that this combination of elements recapitulates the matrix of the mother-child relationship of the early months of life. Moser relates (p. 40, 1977):

However, here comes a memory right out of the playpen—
yet endowed with the imaginative powers of one at least
twelve months old: indeed it was the first affective perception of a rival on the couch. . . . I cannot remember if I
perceived the fellow before me as a person at all, but as soon
as I lay down on the couch, I had the notion that I was lying
in a warm puddle of urine. This was so unpleasant that I
went into the most bizarre contortions in order to stay close
to the edge of the bed, and to spare most of my posterior
surface from the sensation of sticky wetness. It goes without
saying that I complained and blasphemed a lot, but to no
avail. . . . It was not, in any case, possible to deny the exist-
ance of siblings any longer. My perception of them did,
however, occur accompanied with qualities of feeling cus-
tomery among infants. . . . The person to whom I attributed
the urine, on the grounds of some residual warmth on the
couch surface, became my first younger sibling in analysis,
and if one chooses to reverse the projection, it could well be
that my feeling was a cover-up for the wish to drown him in
my own urine.

Menninger (1958) has pointed out that in treatment
there are three main mental areas which are available for
exploration: that of the patient's childhood, the analytic
situation or sessions with the analyst, and the patient's
"outside" reality or daily functioning. He very convincingly
shows that regression is a most important aspect of the
psychoanalytic treatment and one that can connect all three
areas. Regression connects these three areas because it is
the common denominater of the traumatic or deprived
childhood situation, its repetition in terms of the conflicts
found in every day functioning, and its reenactment with
the analyst in the treatment session in terms of the transference. The couch then as described here, is a catalyst in the
induction of a monitored therapeutically useful clinical
regression.

An example of this altered state of inner awareness is
a patient who had been brought up in a number of austere
private boarding schools during latency and adolescence.

He was in one of these schools which emphasized discipline between the ages of 12 and 17. Except for that period in his bed alone at night before falling to sleep, he felt he had no time for himself or his own thoughts. For him the couch represented a delightful period of freedom to let his thoughts and feelings soar unbound, as they did in the prelude to sleep.

For one young, borderline schizophrenic male, fantasies were his only early source of fulfillment. The restrictions of his childhood had otherwise deprived him of practically all forms of self-expression, self-assertion, and consequently his own ego integrity. On the couch he was able to experience his early fantasies, attain relief from his anxieties, and make excellent progress in his treatment.

In addition to the regressive aspects of the phenomena induced by the couch, there are a number of other feelings and ideational states that can be promoted by the analytic setting. Many individuals, particularly in the adolescent years, develop a capacity for day dreaming in the hypnogogic states that precede their falling asleep at night. These states which most people occasionally experience tend to be dreamlike and usually very rich in symbolic meanings. They represent an abandonment to the luxuries of the imagination.

# Chapter 7

# THE RECUMBENT POSITION AND
# ITS RELATION TO SLEEP

The subject of sleep has received a considerable amount of attention in the literature of the theory of psychoanalysis. Because the recumbent position is associated both mentally and physically with sleep, it merits some attention here.

Macalpine (1950) and Lewin (1973) believe that the use of the supine position and free association is an invitation to regress toward primary process and the dream. Macalpine (1950) and Spitz (1956) also indicate that the diminuation of external stimuli, the fact that the patient does not see the analyst, that the analyst is relatively silent, and that there is no physical contact between them furthers a sleep-like state. Ferenczi (1926) wrote about this matter in his early papers. He sees the complaint of being sleepy as a threat to go to sleep, representing dissatisfaction with an aimless, tiresome treatment. He also describes a patient's dream as a fantasy of being overpowered by the analyst during sleep.

Isakower (1936) examines the behavior of the ego in the act of falling asleep. He mainly sees sleep in anlaysis as a regressive phenomenon of the ego accompanied by increased self-observation, detachment from experience, and the revival of early ego attitudes. He observes that in certain patients there were mental images of suckling at the mother's breast, then falling asleep when satisfied. He sees this regressive phenomenon as a disturbance in the normal process of falling asleep.

Simmel (1942, p. 66) views sleep as a defensive mechanism that protects the ego against erotic and aggressive instinctual demands: "In the course of psychoanalytic treatments, we observe patients becoming tired, drowsy, and even falling asleep as a defense against aggressive impulses toward the analyst."

Jekels (1945), following a parallel between sleep and schizophrenia, sees that sleep with its loss of ego feeling can be experienced as dying. He describes semantic associations of sleep with death and refers to the myth of Hermes as "sleepbringer" and the "escort of the dead."

Lewin (1973) remarks that sleep can repeat an oral infantile situation associated with being a satiated nurseling. He theorizes that one form of neurotic fear of sleep is based on a fear of death: a defense against a death-wish in order to achieve union with the idealized infantile mother. Also, he believes that the desire to sleep may coincide with the wish to be eaten: the child's identification with the breast.

Gabe (1951) describes a case of a patient with an obsessive fear of death where falling asleep during the analytic hour is a major transference resistance. He found that in treatment sleeping serves multiple purposes. It wards off homosexual drives and also represents surrender to them; it inhibits discharge of aggressive impulses, but expresses fantasied destructive wishes against love objects. To sleep also satisfied deep oral longings and reunion with the mother.

Dosuzkov (1952) sees sleep during a session as an unmistakable symptom of instinctual dissatisfaction with analysis (in respect to transference). During sessions, one of his patients would talk disconnectedly, stop, then start to snore. Once he awoke and rushed to the bathroom (barely in time) to urinate. Finally, he urinated in bed (at home). Dosuzkov explains that the compulsive sleep during the sessions was the acting out of a childhood neurosis situation, the memory of which was repressed.

Scott (1952, 1956) in two significant papers discussing sleep during psychoanalysis, hypothesizes that the total satisfaction of sleep is waking or the act of waking up. Usually the inference is that the aim is sleep and more sleep. He thinks that when sleepiness or sleep appears in analysis as a regressive defense, the primary wish to sleep is reactivated since there is in most patients evidence of sleep deprivation. Scott states that the analysis of these sleep patterns results in a stage of sleep occurring during interviews followed by subsequent improved ability to sleep between sessions. He believes that analytic progress is hastened rather than slowed by this phenomenon which sometimes results in sleep during psychoanalysis. Another conclusion he reaches is that "blankness" while awake and "nothing to talk about" are sometimes defenses against sleep or sleepiness. He indicates that the activation, analysis, and resolution of these defenses benefit the treatment.

In a more recent unpublished communication, Scott (1971) develops a further series of propositions, some of which are especially of interest to this subject. They are stated briefly as follows:

Sleep is an instinctual drive whose aim is satisfaction. A preconscious part of the wish to awake.

Waking may be repressed and patients may act unconsciously as if they are awake and elsewhere than where they are.

Repression of the wish to sleep itself may lead to many types of displacement, substitution, symbolism, or part function standing for the whole function.

Certain wishes may be based on the frequency with which sleep follows satisfactory early feeding.

To be sleeping with a person or to be with a person who sleeps has transference and counter-transference implications related to: a) taboos against dreaming of patients, b) sleeping during sessions.

Possible criteria for the satisfactory termination of analysis might include adequate working through of the wish to sleep, control of going to sleep, waking and duration, and the depreciation and overvaluation of sleep and dreams.

Parkin (1955) in an intense investigation of two analytic sessions during which a patient slept illustrates the over-determination involved in this act. He says the ego's contribution to this act of sleeping is the wish to produce free associations while in a state of reverie and the wish to dream rather than hallucinate. He shows too how the id contributed to the act through phallic, anal, and oral strivings.

Dickes (1965) in speaking of altered states of consciousness says that sleep in analysis is a defense against emergence of affect related to special sexual and aggressive events in the patient's life. He believes these phenomena also develop as a defense, however unsatisfactory, against external aggression. Intellectual dulling is also related to sleep and is a condition of partial sleep with similar defenses. Dickes also considers drowsiness as the analyst's defense against aggression, a manifestation of counter-transference. Boredom is explained as a high state of instinctual tension with little opportunity for release. He believes that boredom produces a situation favorable to the development of regressive fantasies and feeling. Analysts are in a special position to become victims of these phenomena.

Dean (1957) also investigates drowsiness as counter-transference. He concludes this drowsiness is principally the analyst's response to his patients' aggressiveness. It is his defense against feelings of powerlessness and discouragement.

Freud (1914b) examines sleep as one of the primary regressive states. He believes the object of sleeping is to attain the state of sleep itself as a fulfillment of the wish to sleep. He later writes (1917b) that the change from totally self-sufficient narcissism to a condition in which the changing outer world produces pain cannot be suffered for long, and sleep is used as a defense against such pain.

No author studied has as intensively explored the profound and sophisticated relationship that exists between the meaning and use of the couch and the actual and symbolic aspects of sleeping and dreaming as has Lewin (1973). His thoughts on this subject have been so extensive and far-ranging and of such fine quality that a survey of his writings must necessarily go beyond summarizing and paraphrasing to include direct quotes at some length.

He (p. 264) clearly states the equation he perceives between the "couch" and what he calls the "analytic situation" as follows:

> . . . the analytic situation, which is here defined, empirically, as the familiar standard hour, or loosely, as "what happens on the couch"; and sometimes the word "couch" will be used metaphorically as synonymous with "analytic situation". Included in the idea of analytic situation are the phenomena of free association, resistance, transference, repetition, and others well known and generally admitted as working concepts.

Not only does Lewin equate the couch with the analytic situation, but also with the couch and sleeping. He (p. 271) further makes a connection between sleeping and dying:

At this point, however, I should merely like to emphasize once more the natural unconscious equivalence of sleep and death, both of them states of narcissism, psychologically. Also that the exception to the narcissism of death, to wit, the afterlife. But more to the present purpose, I wish to indicate by these examples the sort of resistance there might be to lying down on the analytic couch, and how the couch and the analytic situation itself need interpretation. In all its variety the most obvious interpretation, not necessarily the deepest, is that the couch is a place for sleeping.

In discussing the resistances to the use of the couch, he (pp. 270, 243) investigates the fear connected with death:

I shall merely name some of the pregenital varieties of the fear of death, or the fear of being put to sleep which is the same. These are: the fear of being devoured, of being poisoned, of being suffocated; and finally, a variety which is not so much a fear of dying in the sense of losing consciousness (sleeping) as a fear of the afterlife (and bad dreams), a fear rather ignored in our materialistic era.

One sometimes encounters a fear of being asleep on the couch, which is related to a fear of dreaming.

He (pp. 283, 290) makes a link between the feelings accompanying association while on the couch and conditions in the dreams:

Affects on the couch or arising during solitary association are like those that appear in dreams. They are part of the manifest content. The Freudian intention is to analyze them, as in dream analysis determine whether a "happy mood" may not conceal a fear of death, or whether an anxiety is a signal and a repetition. The solitary meditator may take the affect at its face manifest value and go on from there, taking the elated and depressed feelings especially as warranted.

It will be noted that the analyst is at both ends and around the diagram of the psychic apparatus; that he is "around" the couch as the external world is around the dream.

The rest of the mapping on to the couch of dream psychology is not difficult, for "analysis-formation" is like dream formation and involves the same memory traces and psychic systems, though usually in different proportions. Blank dreams are approximated by the "blank couch," that is, sleep on the couch where the narcissism of sleep which is "under" the dream comes out into the open as "couch narcissism."

Again in the following statement Lewin (pp. 242–243) equates the bed and the couch:

Many associations refer to the similarity of bed and couch, and some patients reproduce the process of going to sleep, occasionally including the characteristic Isakower phenomena. Again with many patients the couch as bed and hence an early substitute and symbol for the mother, enters into the transference situation, for the analyst's remarks become the equivalent of the noises and wakers, and are equated with the father's or superego's wakening and weaning injunctions (Stone, 1947). Thus it happens that patients oral problems may automatically react to the noise they must ignore.

His writings (pp. 243–244) contain many examples of the meaning his couch has to his patients as illustrated here:

The equation of the analytic work to being in bed is very evident in some patients. Years ago, a patient made a remark which I have always remembered but apparently did not fully understand at the time. Toward the end of her analysis she went to her physician for a physical examination. To his surprise he found that gastric ulcer of some years' standing had healed, and he asked her what she had been doing for it. "Oh," she said, "I have been lying down for an hour every afternoon." This was a joke; it was long before the term psychosomatic had gained popularity, and I was amused.

Retrospectively, I see that she was stating a deep analytic verity, one particularly clear to me since Stone's (1947) report of the doudenal ulcer patient who fell asleep on the couch. My patient is the one I referred to in my paper on claustrophobia, who assumed the "foetal posture" on the couch and anxiously blurted out "Don't touch me!" Her conflict was between her genital wishes and her attachment to her mother, and she was saying to me (ambivalently), "Don't wean or waken me!". But her joke was psychologically penetrating; her ulcer had been cured by "lying down" by a form of therapy which enabled her to relive and understand infantile sleep.

A male patient could not lie down for several months at the beginning of this analysis. Finally, he lay down with marked pleasure, rationalized as a realistic triumph, but which was certainly also a libidinal repetition, for, as he told me many times, his life and his analysis involved a constant struggle against spending all his time in sleep. The ability to assume the recumbent posture was not the brilliant technical achievement it might seem; for long after he was settled on the couch, he came to realize that he automatically "closed his ears" to what I said to him, as if to guard against being disturbed in his sleep, and after an upsetting analytic session he would often react by taking a nap.

Lewin (p. 241–242) shows that for some patients treatment on the couch is associated with being hypnotically asleep:

> . . . But if we ask why the hypnotist used the couch, we come upon the obvious reason: to accommodate the patient hypnotically asleep. Many of our patients remark on, or indicate, the suggestible effect of lying down. I do not refer to those who go to sleep. Many others take the couch as a bed for sleeping, for dreaming, or for dormescent fantasy; they loosen their clothing, take off their glasses and ornaments, perhaps kick off their shoes, or they make other trivial and abortive preparations for sleep. They complain or comment pleasantly on the pillow and the mattress, and sometimes bring a bed into their initial transference dreams. On the psychological level, our patients assume with us that what they say on the couch is not to be taken as a sworn statement of a fully aroused and critical person, but more like what they are apt to think of when they are alone and relaxed, as when they are in bed.

## THE USE OF THE COUCH AND THE FEAR OF SLEEPING

Many people, both patients and therapists, are afraid of falling asleep during treatment. They prefer to sit up rather than use the couch and succumb to their fear of falling asleep and the defenses against it. All the thoughts and feelings people have pertaining to this phenomenon are actually valid and usable aspects of the psychoanalytic process.

Concern about falling asleep has been evident from the beginnings of psychoanalysis, and there have been many investigations of this phenomenon. What has not been sufficiently investigated in these studies of sleep and its meaning in therapy is the problem of analysts as well as patients falling asleep, especially in connection with the use of the couch.

For the patient, fear of sleeping on the couch in the treatment session can be two-fold. It can be concerned with fear of falling asleep himself or fear of his analyst falling asleep. These fears can have several sources: The patient's latent, preconscious fears can be enhanced by previously heard jokes, stories, and cartoons that depict the couch as a place for napping.

Just as popular humor shows the patient asleep on the couch, so too is the analyst often depicted as snoozing in his chair behind the patient. This provides substance to the fear that the analyst might fall asleep. These fears are usually based upon one or more beliefs that the analyst's sleeping signifies:

a) that rather than doing his job of listening, the analyst is cheating the patient,
b) that there is lack of feeling and concern for the patient,
c) that the patient's contribution to the relationship is not worthwhile, and he is inadequate,

d)   that the analyst would like to get rid of him, and
e)   that he is being ridiculed by the analyst.

Many of such fears and beliefs are derivatives of un-resolved conflicts stemming from frustrating childhood sit-uations. Others are based upon personal experiences or those related by others where a therapist falls asleep during treatment sessions or where the therapist conveys un-friendly or uncaring attitudes to patients. Whatever the source, the feeling of being unwanted or inadequate can be focused upon almost any aspect of the treatment, and the analyst's being out of sight can serve as a screen for these feelings.

On an unconscious level, a patient may have oral fears of losing the maternal breast and of being abandoned. Sleep on the couch can represent that state to which the infant has yielded after much frustration and fruitless cry-ing for attention or nourishment. With the therapist/mother out of sight, hope is abandoned and the relief of sleep is sought. As long as the therapist can be seen, the hope for comfort and nourishment exists for certain peo-ple. Thus, looking at the therapist is protection against the fear of abandonment.

Certain patients connect sleep with psychosis. It is a time when their egos are less attached to reality, when their most fearful fantasies are being played out. They implore relief from these fantasies but are forced back into them when they seek relief from a reality which is also intolera-ble. The author treated a woman who entered analysis after her third suicide attempt. She could not bear to be alone. Only as long as she saw me did I exist. When alone she obsessively engaged in much masturbation with much guilt. As a child she was often rebuked for not being willing to play by herself. Later, sexually playing with herself was forbidden and brought forth much guilt. Her usual fanta-sies connected with masturbation were painful and shameful episodes of being sexually exploited by others. While engaging in these fantasies she would drift in and out of sleep. But, lying on the couch during the analytic hour he. sexual feelings would mount, and she would go into an anxiety state feeling out of touch, alone, guilty, with sleep as something to be desired and yet feared.

Small children, as evidenced by their nightmares, also often fear sleep. It is perceived as a state of helplessness and vulnerability. It is a time when monsters can get at them. After playing, fighting, and other daytime activities, children are often asked in the evenings to give up all this and go to bed. They are obliged in doing this to relinquish physical activities and replace them with mental activities such as fantasy and dreaming. Instead of behaving in an active way they now engage in passively feeling, thinking, and recollecting. For many children who are very active all day, their bed is their only place for exclusively mental activity. Many children rebel against having to relinquish their daytime activities and regard sleep and napping in a most unwelcome way. At the same time this passive way of reflecting trains them, by their conditioning, to fall asleep.

At an anal level people can be concerned about wasting time and money. Talk is a useful product, while sleep is waste matter. There can be anal sadistic fantasies of being sexually penetrated while asleep. To the patient, the regressive phenomenon of sleep can represent the loss of control of one's fate and of being subject to the will of another person. It can also be the fear of loss of control over one's own body with resulting shame from soiling.

A male patient complained about using the couch, fearing that he would fall asleep and that this would waste time and money. He reported that during previous sessions with another therapist when such a state of sleep was beginning to overcome him, he was startled into complete wakefulness by a sudden fear he was about to be anally penetrated. As a child he had feared his mother's seductiveness and had often been enraged at her excessive familiarity with his body. She treated him as her object to which she had access at her pleasure.

On a phallic level, sleep can represent directly sexual activity. Both in the English language and in others, "to sleep" with someone implies to have sexual contact with them. For many people the solitary moments in their own bed are the only times they allow themselves sexual thoughts, feelings, and activity. For them, to sleep in someone's presence can represent a form of sexual contact which is threatening.

A young woman of high moral principles who led a solitary life could never lie still on the couch but would writhe and often turn around. For a long time she objected to using the couch because of her need to look. Her movements on the couch turned out to be a compromise between her wish for physical closeness and objection to sleeping with someone unless she was married to him.

In another instance, on observing that a patient was squeezing the sides of the couch the author questioned him about this. He said, "When you asked that, an image of breasts came into my mind. Actually the idea of squeezing a penis came into my mind, but I didn't want to say it. I suppose I didn't want to say it because it is safer to say breasts than penis." The patient went on to recall that as an adolescent he would masturbate by lying on his stomach on a pillow and rocking back and forth while squeezing the pillow. He recalled with some embarrassment that he once walked into his adolescent son's room while the son was masturbating in the same fashion. Then he asked how he should react to his son compulsively fondling his penis in front of him. After a discussion of this, he then released his grip on the couch and stated he was suddenly feeling very relaxed. "Whatever we talked about seems to have relaxed me. My hands are hanging down freely."

It is usually helpful and reassuring to analysands to be told it is all right for them to fall asleep during their sessions. In fact for them to fall asleep might be beneficial as it would indicate they were sufficiently relaxed and secure in the analysts presence to permit sleep. To fall asleep it is usually necessary to feel sleepy, and this feeling is needed at some point in the treatment to assure a healthy outcome. With this reassurance most people do proceed to relax, but it is rare for them to fall asleep.

In reviewing the literature, it becomes evident that while much is written about the meaning of patients sleeping during treatment, relatively little is said about the analyst sleeping. More open examination of this topic may alleviate some of the fear that is attached to this concern about sleeping.

In addition to any direct implication created in the patient's mind by the idea of the analyst slumbering during the session, most therapists are concerned about their image within their professional community. They fear falling asleep because they believe it would affect their prestige. Disparaging remarks have been made about analysts who have been discovered fast asleep. This fear of falling asleep has led in some instances to the implementation of a number of defensive patterns. Not only do some therapists have their patients sit up to maintain their own alertness, but instances are known where some therapists have also sought teaching and hospital and clinic staff positions in order to break the routine of an otherwise long day of consecutively working with patients. Other therapists have found group therapy a way of diluting the strain of trying to maintain a wakeful relaxed state while listening for many hours to persons on the couch. For them a group situation provides more excitement. Some resort to coffee drinking and even drug stimulants to stay awake.

In general the idea of a therapist sleeping in treatment is frowned upon. Fromm-Reichmann (1950) sees many reasons for avoiding the use of the couch with the therapist seated behind it. One major reason is that she believes this kind of relationship opens the door too widely to the possibility of the therapist napping during the patient's sessions. She (p. 68) states; "The classical psychoanalytic setup of the doctor sitting behind the patient, who is lying on the couch, may imply the danger of encouraging any inclination on the part of the psychiatrist to drowse."

This kind of attitude is based upon the belief that analysts are like airtraffic controllers, expected to be awake, alert, and listening to all communications. That this may not always be true of them seems to elicit anxiety and guilt in the analyst and fear and anger in the patient. In any case, this belief is based upon a view of the analyst's function that reflects the conventional view of person-to-person communication, overtly reacting to every stimulus.

For the analyst, however, the shortest line is not necessarily that one between two points which is typical of logical thought processes. In analysis such rational landmarks do not exist. To arrive at his understanding, he may have to utilize not only the patient's thoughts, feelings, and memory, but also his own. He often relies upon his intuition as well as his knowledge and training. When he listens, it may be beyond the ordinary dimensions, with what Reik (1948) calls, "the third ear." The analyst examines the patient's dreams and fantasies, and often his own in addition. Menninger (1958, p. 87) writes:

> Theoretically, he (the analyst) has merely to observe the effect on the role he plays as a silent listener and apparent frustrator upon the suppliant party. They are both participants in this process, and notwithstanding the fact that the patient is consciously and undeniably frustrated in the analytic situation whereas the analyst is theoretically not frustrated, what we all realize is that to some extent the patient is gratified and the analyst is frustrated. Correspondingly, the analyst, as a human being, reacts to his frustrations and makes use of various "defense" measures, particularly identification and projection. He, too, undergoes waves of temporary regression, including temporary misidentification of

his patient. His patient momentarily becomes his mother, his father, a pupil, a colleague, another patient, or even a projection of the analyst's own self.

Earlier Ferenczi (1919, p. 70) also commented on this process:

Analytic therapy, therefore, makes claims on the doctor that seem directly self-contradictory. On the one hand, it requires of him the free play of association and phantasy, the full indulgence of his own unconscious: we know from Freud that only in this way is it possible to grasp intuitively the expressions of the patient's unconscious that are concealed in the manifest material of the manner of speech and behavior. On the other hand, the doctor must subject the material submitted by himself and the patient to a logical scrutiny, and in his dealings and communications may only let himself be guided exclusively by the result of this mental effort. In time one learns to interrupt and letting oneself go on certain signals from the preconscious, and to put the critical attitude in its place. This constant oscillation between the free play of phantasy and critical scrutinizing presupposes a freedom and uninhibited motility of psychic excitation on the doctor's part, however, that can hardly be demanded in any other sphere.

Freud (1912a) believes it best for the analyst to maintain a posture of free-floating attention permitting the analyst's attention to range from the patient to himself, in terms of thoughts, feelings, dreams, and fantasies, and back to the patient again. To achieve this the analyst must have a fair amount of freedom, both intellectually, emotionally, and to some extent physically. Intellectual freedom includes the opportunity to think through the material that develops during the session, to allow his fantasies and feelings to roam, to ponder the meaning of the various communications evolving from the relationship, and to be able to express to the patient, when appropriate, understanding that has developed from this process.

Another kind of freedom the analyst requires is the physical freedom offered by positioning his chair behind the couch. Optimally, it permits the analyst to examine the patient's activities and also his own without interfering with the patient's communications. It permits him to stretch and change position during long hours of sitting without distracting his patient. It allows him to close his eyes and concentrate on external stimuli as well as his own inner communications without being impolite. How can a treatment requiring the utilization of a highly-trained professional person's time, ability, and effectiveness to the fullest extent also allow him to cope with his own human needs? The analyst is bombarded with stimuli that magnify ordinary needs to even greater heights. Being physically restricted and subjected to daily, continuous discussions involving anger, sex, and tragedy, the analyst can internalize considerable stress, which he can hope to minimize by making his environment as comfortable as possible.

Another factor influencing the amount of tension that is experienced during the course of a working day is the amount of sleep obtained the previous night. As incongruous as it may appear, too much sleep is not always to the analyst's advantage. It leaves him too wide awake and too ready for physical activity, an outlet simply not available to a busy therapist. A sleep deficiency that can be satisfied gradually from the deeply restful physical state he maintains during the day is more suitable to the passive work the analyst does. But naturally, this twilight state can carry the therapist close to the edge that separates being awake from being asleep. It provides a greater opportunity to fall asleep: the very condition that is both his and the patient's fear. There is reason to believe that less than full attention on the part of the analyst is not necessarily of great detriment to the treatment.

Ferenczi (1926, p. 103) has commented upon this:

The fact that the doctor at many interviews pays little heed to the patient's associations and only pricks up his ears at certain statements also belongs to the chapter on "Counter-transference"; Subsequent scrutiny mostly shows that we were reacting unconsciously to the emptiness and worthless-ness of the associations just presented by the withdrawal of conscious excitation; at the first idea of the patient's that in any way concerns the treatment, we brighten up again. The danger, therefore, of the doctor falling asleep and leaving the patient unobserved is not great. (I owe the full confirma-tion of the observation to a verbal discussion of the subject with Prof. Freud.)

Much more blunt in his permissive attitude toward the therapist's sleeping is Perls (1969, p. 79) who carries this tolerence to the extreme:

So, whenever you get bored or tense, always withdraw—if you fall asleep when the patient doesn't bring any interest-ing things, it saves your strength, and the patient will either wake you up or come back with some more interesting mate-rial. And if not, you at least have time for a snooze.

The worth of a patient's communication as a justifica-tion for whether or not the analyst may doze seems a dubi-ous criterion for such a position. As the subsequent discussion on counter-transference will explain, it can be that the very moment the patient's verbalizing is most meaningful, the analyst may be inclined to fall asleep. It can be the more powerful feelings in the relationship that lead the therapist into slumber.

Falling asleep during a session is a hazard of the pro-fession that should be minimized. Although it can happen, the likelihood of the analyst's falling asleep in the presence of any one patient more than once is small. Should he find himself tending to slumber, the analyst should consider possible subjective counter-resistance factors and a need to expand his sleep patterns at night, and should also use periods between patients to rest himself in his chair or couch. If sleepiness occurs with any frequency with a particular patient, the counter-transference resistances should be thoroughly investigated.

Concerning counter-transference, a number of writers observe that they use feelings induced in them by their patients to provide understanding of the therapeutic process in their relationship with their patients (Rosenfeld, 1952; Racker, 1957). Spotnitz (1969) calls these feelings induced in the analyst by the patient "objective counter-transference feelings." He states that they can be utilized and developed into a precise tool capable of resolving emotional resistances in patients. He explains that another form of counter-transference, "subjective counter-transference," lies outside of the patient's influence upon the analyst. Thus, sleepiness as a result of the patient's repressed anger would be considered objective counter-transference resistance. The task of the analyst when sleepiness occurs is to examine the source of his feelings. If it is subjective resistance, that is, any factors originating with the analyst and interfering with his task of understanding and analyzing the patient, it should be dealt with by practical means. It should be studied and understood so that it can be resolved. An investigative attitude is one of the most positive ones in moving the treatment forward.

My own experiences and discussions with other analysts indicates it is rare to find someone who has never fallen asleep during the analytic hour. Depending upon the feelings, especially narcissistic ones being communicated, one's health at the time, and the length of the day, and the inclination to sleep is affected. An additional variable is certain counter-transference elements in the therapist's own life that are defended against by a feeling of sleepiness. The realization of having napped is usually met with surprise. What is further surprising is that the sleeping was of only a few minutes duration but seemed longer. Also observed have been patterns of sleepiness occuring at certain periods of the day and with certain patients. Contrary to what might be expected these patients seem to make progress equivalent to the others with whom the analyst is wide awake. This observation, however, is consistant with the view that it is not what the analyst says that heals the patient but rather what the patient says.

Avoidance of the use of the couch either when initiated by the patient or the analyst as a cautionary measure against sleeping can be an unfortunate loss of an opportunity to explore another dimension in the treatment process. If this is done out of some kind of fear or wish, every effort should first be made to investigate this.

If the use of the couch is to be abandoned due to the pressure of sleep needs, it can be determined whether the sleep wish can be temporarily gratified while recommending ways of getting more adequate amounts of sleep prior to sessions. Basically, however, the problem of sleep should not be a main consideration in whether or not the psychoanalytic *couch* is utilized as a treatment instrument.

*Chapter 8*

# THE USE OF THE COUCH TO FACILITATE RELAXATION AND THE EXPRESSION OF FEELINGS

Some aspects of psychoanalytic theory seem to run parallel to principles of physiological functioning. For example, sleep is not only a vital psychological necessity, but seems to be an important physiological one as well. Sleep is not only a form of mental relaxation but is also one of physical regression. These parallels have relevance to the use of the couch in the sense that the couch fosters physical as well as psychological regression with an interplay of one upon the other. Physiological regression seems to promote emotional regression.

The late Norwegian psychoanalyst, Trygve Braatøy (1954), focused his attention on the physical aspects of the recumbent position. He believed that relaxation on the couch and the break with everyday conventions made it easier for the "wisdom of the body to express itself." He felt that physiological considerations were of great importance. Braatøy discussed this aspect of the couch in great detail as well as the so-called psychological aspects and indeed, they deserve some review, since he is one of the few writers who has devoted considerable attention to the use of the couch. The following provides some indication of his thoughts:

> The couch acts by taking away that part of the postural rigidity or tension in the patient's muscles which in a standing or sitting position is necessary in overcoming the force of gravity. It makes him literally more pliant and more responsive to the analyst's suggestion. For this reason the couch has its risks. These risks are, as one sees, directly related to the couch being a common factor in hypnotic and psychoanalytic treatment. If, however, the therapist does not exploit this possibility, but sticks to an unbiased, questioning attitude, continues to be interested in the patient's individuality and spontaneity, the relaxation on the couch gives him a specific opportunity to observe the blocking of spontaneous movement determined by experience outside the analytic situation. (p. 119)

> In relation to the somatic influence of the couch, the arguments can be examined in this way: it is easy to call forth rumbling in the guts—"make them talk"—if the patient relaxes in a supine position. It is more difficult if he is sitting up, and practically impossible if he is standing. (p. 154)

> If we agree that some chronic neurotics have experienced fundamental and formative frustrations in preverbal periods, a reasonable technical conclusion is that our technique must include non-verbal approaches. The couch is such a non-verbal instrument. In its posture-releasing capacity it helps to release respiration and by that emotion. (p. 236)

> On a biological background one understands the mind as a function of the body. In clinical work one discovers that repression, inhibition, defense, and resistance mean bodily tensions. (p. 117)

> Seeing this, the analyst will further discover that the influence of the patient's attitudes and postures—as far as these are determined by situation—inadequate tension—are essential in understanding how psychoanalysis acts. It acts by changing the attitude (posture) of the patient. (p. 117)

> This (physio)therapeutic work has always been an integral
> part of psychoanalysis. In classic psychoanalysis it goes on
> from the beginning of the first analytic hour to the end of
> the last with the help of the couch. (p. 119)

Braatøy very interestingly equates change of attitude
with change of posture, i.e., from the upright to the supine
position. He also places such abstract analytic concepts as
repression, inhibition, defense, and resistance concretely
in the body and relates these mechanisms to bodily tensions. It is likely that such assertions will be challenged
since they are not readily demonstrable. Nevertheless, bed
rest as an antidote for physical tensions is an age-old remedy.

In a reclining position a person's pulse is likely to slow
down, the body musculature tends to become more flaccid,
and the breathing is likely to become slower, deeper, and
more even. With this usually comes a relaxation that assists
the entire process of awareness so that the patient becomes
more alert than he normally is to feelings, thoughts, and his
own words. In time this activity contributes to the development of an observing ego. As this process of relaxation
continues the patient himself becomes increasingly aware
of his censoring and other holding back tendencies, and
what was involuntary tends to become voluntary. A patient
once related: "When I come in, I'm usually in a panic.
Lying down and relaxing I can sort things out and get them
in perspective. Somehow I get myself calmed down and I
can walk out relaxed."

One senses in Braatøy a deep respect for the patient's
spontaneity. He believes that the passivity of the analytic
situation which utilizes the couch serves to cultivate and
nourish this spontaneity. He (p. 108) says:

> The passivity in the analytic situation—including the pa-
> tient's supine position on the couch, undisturbed by the
> analyst's face play—contains a cultivation of a deep respect

for the nervous individual's spontaneity (personality). This respect was voiced as a clarion call to the future of psychotherapy when the distinguished, middle-aged Vienna internist Joseph Breuer accepted that a young hysterical girl was "completely unsuggestible" and for this reason gave up suggestions in the form of commandments or postulates, and changed his approach to arguments based on what she said or showed.

Verbal spontaneity is encouraged by gradually reducing the fear of an action which might produce an unpleasant result. As the patient learns on the couch to convert feelings, thoughts, and intentions into the safety of words, rather than actions, greater possibilities for creative thought begin to materialize. The patient's spontaneity is seen as his part of the therapeutic activity and the analyst's encouragement of this spontaneity mutually contribute toward a cure.

Because Braatøy is sensitive to the possibility that an overzealous therapist might urge tasks upon his patient before he, the therapist, thoroughly understands the complexity of the situation. Braatøy (p. 117) cautions the analyst to pay close attention to the patient's physical state in order to assess the patient's readiness for a task or interpretation.

## RELAXATION

The condition of relaxation which is induced by the setting, the attitude of the analyst, and by the use of the recumbent position has a definite place in psychoanalytic theory.

Relaxation is a state of feeling that is characterized by a tolerance of fantasies and external perceptions, and relative harmony between the ego, superego, id, and external reality. It is a generally pleasurable state that is tension-free and is reflected in the body musculature, which is also tension-free. This is not to say that no effort is being exerted because the individual is seeking to either actively or passively accomplish something. However, the activity will be within the conflict-free sphere of the ego. Levels of cathexis that are high, tending toward the discharge of sexual or aggressive energies at a rapid rate, and are strong counter-cathexis are not likely to be consistent with relaxation. While instinctual pressure for discharge is not consistent with relaxation, the ego, nevertheless, must be capable of binding these energies, delaying and managing their discharge, accepting substitutes when necessary, and tolerating frustration.

The ability to relax can be a very efficient mechanism of the total personality. A relative tolerance for fantasy or its derivatives and the diminuation of strong countercathexis is essential to relaxation, at least at the beginning phase of most activities. Sex and creative efforts can suffer if a state of relaxation does not exist initially.

Difficulty in relaxing can result from high levels of guilt, anxiety, and environmental or instinctual pressure. An inability to relax can be a symptom of any psychoneurosis. This inability is most clearly in evidence when there are no specific duties or activities which need to be performed. In general the ability to relax probably infers some degree of optimism at an oral, libidinal level that includes a promise of some ultimate gratification.

While the use of the reclining position is intended to provide an optimum condition for relaxing, it also can allow the exploration of those feelings that interfere with a state of relaxation.

Feelings are evoked by stimuli that are either external or internal in origin. An individual's image of the external world is formed through the sense organ perceptions. The individual learns that he is hungry, thirsty, sleepy, or tired through inner perception. Although it may be impossible for him to prove the existence of the external world, he is usually able (unless he is extremely ill emotionally) to differentiate between sense organ perception and the world of fantasy.

It is possible to control or eliminate certain stimuli voluntarily (e.g., closing the eyes). In general, however, awareness of external and internal stimuli takes place automatically. Because this process occurs automatically it is sometimes very difficult for the ego, even under normal conditions, to question the source of the information received. The awareness of the presence of certain sensations that may be caused by either internal or external stimuli can often be consciously avoided by suppression. Suppression is an ego mechanism in which the awareness of a sensation can, as a result of a decision, be voluntarily eliminated. On the other hand, repression and denial are ego mechanisms by which the individual avoids conscious awareness of certain sensations without consciously making such a decision. Suppression, repression, or denial do not serve to eliminate the stimulus; they merely prevent the knowledge or awareness of the sensation caused by the stimulus from becoming conscious.

If one subscribes to the idea that feelings as well as thoughts are of significance for the treatment, it follows that the recumbent position, since it induces a greater amount of relaxation for most people and provides contrasting alterations in emotional states, has many advantages. When we are working with character disorders that are known to be particularly difficult to treat, inhibited emotions can be revealed not only by the way the patient speaks but also by the way he presents himself physically on the couch. Wilhelm Reich (1949) was very concerned with this problem. He believed that the physical posturing is an emotional expression and that unloosening the emotional binds can only come through releasing physical tensions which are bound in what he calls the body armor. Reich's observations (p. 41) are as follows:

Inhibition of aggression and psychic armouring go hand in hand with an increased tonus, even a rigidity of the musculature. Affect-blocked patients lie on the couch, stiff as a board, without any motion. It is difficult to eliminate this muscular tension. If one lets the patient relax consciously, the muscular tension is replaced by restlessness. In other cases patients carry out various unconscious movements, and when these are stopped, anxious sensations immediately make their appearance.

He (p. 343) amplifies this further:

One finds very often that the state of muscular tension is different before the solution of an acute repression and afterwards. When patients are in an acute resistance, that is, when they try to keep an idea or an impulse from consciousness, they often feel a tension, say, in the head, the thighs or the buttocks. After having overcome the resistance, they suddenly feel relaxed. One patient said in such a situation, "I feel as if I had had sexual gratification."

Reich discusses the connections between physical states and emotional states which he and other observers have perceived. He illustrates how with emotional change there is physical change. But the patient does not initially know of such things as resistances, nor is he at first aware, accustomed as he is to the routine of his everyday affairs, of the close links between his thoughts, feelings, and physical states. Most analysts have observed the shift toward increasing physical relaxation on the couch in terms of a more flaccid posture, slower and more even breathing, fewer sighs, and a speech pattern that is lower key and more even in tempo, as their apprehensions are revealed, examined, and resolved. Most patients are not initially subjectively aware of their tensions, but realize their absence through increasing relaxation and ensuing comfort. Gradually the link among thoughts, feelings, memories, and physical states is recognized and this becomes for many people a new insight that is generalized to other parts of their lives with great benefit.

## THE EXPRESSION OF FEELINGS

With the diminished distractions offered by the unstimulating analytic setting, most people develop heightened sensitivity to these otherwise almost imperceptible sensations. With good analytic technique they learn to give verbal expression to these otherwise transitory thoughts and feelings and to communicate them. In a world where extreme value is placed upon certain feelings to the almost contemptible exclusion of others, the recapture of the ability to perceive all feelings could be considered as one of the criteria for emotional health (Stern, 1966).

Healthy awareness is crippled when people attach their ability or tendency to feel certain things rather than allow themselves to feel everything and confront the situations that rise to these feelings. This lack of connection between the reality of one's situation and bodily feelings is often pathological. It remains as part of the analytic task to help reestablish these connections. The connections are reestablished by encouraging, through free verbal expressions, a full range of feelings and thoughts including those of early childhood. Stern (p. 146) writes that

> To achieve in psychoanalytic treatment the capacity for the optimum in free association (and feelings) means recapturing that childhood state when reality was almost indistinguishable from fantasy and differences were usually irrelevant.

It means permitting the ego to re-experience certain narcissistic states, at least within the presumably safe confines of the analytic situation and then leading it along a safe path of maturation. Most people recline when they want to relax and analysis benefits from this natural tendency by allowing the reexperiencing and resolution of unresolved conflicts, while simultaneously securing the ego defenses.

A critical period in many an analysis is that time when the rage, which has for so long been focused on the self with ensuing depression and any number of physical symptoms, changes direction and finds outward expression, usually with the analyst as the first transference object. These first attempts are sometimes uncertain, often introduced in the form of dreams, slips, and other symbols. Fearfully testing the ice, the patient may first send forth feeble verbal probes. These initial probes have the main task of testing out the analyst. Spotnitz (1969, p. 78) has written:

> Faithful attendance and adherence to the couch position are less important per se than in their respective contributions to verbal communication. Obviously, the time available for talking is reduced if the patient misses or comes late to his sessions. Use of the couch enables him to communicate whatever he thinks, feels, and remembers with relative freedom from environmental and bodily stimulation. He is in the most favorable physical and psychological state to verbalize his immediate intrapsychic experience when he lies on the couch in a relaxed position, with legs uncrossed and arms at his side. Moreover, the safety factor cannot be disregarded when one is working on the obstacles to the discharge of frustration-aggression. The practioner has had a forewarning of any danger that the patient will behave destructively when his changes of position on the couch can be observed.

An example of this is a patient who began treatment with depression and a large degree of confusion. He lay on the couch many months complaining and whining. Slowly, changes in the sessions began to occur. Long periods of silence began to characterize his hours of treatment.

Slowly, and intermittently, his dreams of someone being hit in a fight, killed in an auto accident, slain in combat, appeared. These dreams frightened him, sometimes making him wake at night in a panic. Cautiously, as though stepping on thin ice, he showed his dissatisfaction with the treatment, then the analyst. These initial efforts were followed by quiet interludes. Apparently the ice held. Then came the full storm of the assault. All those resentments he had been containing surged forth. It left him feeling empty and gasping with the deep breaths his asthma had previously blocked. His sallow cheeks flushed with the glow of the battle. It was a one-man riot on the couch. This recumbent platform seems to have been a very adequate battleground, possibly better than a vis-a-vis position would have been. Visually confronting the analyst as an audience whom he would imagine peering and reacting to various performances could have been very inhibiting. Not seeing the analyst, the patient can only imagine his manner and reactions. Facing the other person as an observer brings into the picture an added element of realistic ego-defense against the release of aggression.

In the analyst's consulting room, ego-defenses appear as resistances. The ego defenses which evolved in the past to protect and preserve the child now find their expression in resistances that operate to impede the treatment due to the belief that the analyst will treat him as other provoking or destructive people out of his past treated him. For example, the patient needs to accept the idea that he can lie on the couch and talk and that no harm will come to him or the analyst. This idea is often met with considerable opposition, for in the lives of many people there was no such isolated activity as just talk. This is difficult to accomplish because the very effort itself to explore these apprehensions is often met with opposition. Part of the difficulty had to do with the fact that words themselves carry over from childhood the magic ability to inspire or instigate action.

The analyst must help decathect from words this magical ability and instead convert them into fuel for conceptual thinking. It is an important step forward when wishes and behavior can be talked about without fear of their automatically being converted into activities to be fearful or ashamed of.

We are all performers in this arena of life and learned long ago to be fearful of the first stated, then implied, then expected remonstrances such as, "Don't act that way," "Act your age," "Stop behaving like a cry baby." Behind the way we do not want to act is the way we fear we will or might be acting, and further back of that is the way we want to act. There are those endless hours of rehearsing how not to act. On the couch patients are more likely to express the fear: "I'm afraid that when you know more about me, you won't like me," and this leads to "I am afraid to express my dissatisfaction with you."

These fears which can be projections onto the analyst can be explained by another of Freud's discoveries, the unconscious compulsion to repeat earlier patterns. These repetitions are blessings and hindrances when manifested in the analytic relationship. They appear in treatment in the form of transference. They are blessings because they portray in the "here and now" an accurate portrait of the formative elements in the patient's personality. They are hindrances in the sense that they are not easily swayed by logic, but more often respond to proper emotional intervention. In either case they are known clinically as resistances. No adequate discussion of psychoanalytic theory can be complete without the understanding of these basic elements of resistance and transference. Since resistances and transference are so basic to psychoanalysis, their dynamics are essential to a proper understanding of the role of the couch. This role which is relevant to psychoanalytic procedure will be discussed in the following chapter.

*Chapter 9*

# TECHNIQUE IN USING THE RECUMBENT POSITION

Theoretical psychoanalysts attempt to understand and explain the principles which govern human behavior and thought. Psychoanalytic technique is the application of psychoanalytic theory to the recognition, understanding, and resolution of human conflict and emotional disorder as they appear in consulting rooms.

Theory building can occur in the absence of technical knowledge. However, technique without knowledge of theory proceeds both dangerously and haphazardly, and with only limited success. Technique in the absence of familiarity with the theory of psychoanalysis becomes a mechanical and sterile intellectual enterprise. Such technique, therefore, lacks the adaptive processes that lead to the creative and progressive changes which may in turn produce successful outcomes in treating emotional disorders.

Many analysts use the couch as a psychoanalytic instrument without being aware of the theory behind its use. Knowing theoretical issues, most particularly those of resistance and transference, allows for the orderly development and implementation of technique that will insure the best possible outcome for the time-consuming and expensive psychoanalytic course of treatment. Optimally, there will be available to the analyst a body of technique that will allow flexibility to his approach in accordance with his understanding of each patient's specific pathological dynamics.

To assert that psychoanalysis can not be conducted except with the use of the couch would be contrary to both historical fact and to the experience of most therapists. As stated earlier, Freud probably analyzed himself both with and without the use of the recumbent position. Farrow (1953) undoubtedly derived considerable benefit from his self-analysis after several unsatisfactory attempts in the classical manner. Ferenczi (1920) utilizing his active method, experimented without the use of the recumbent position with selected patients, as do many of the avant-garde Neo-Freudians. The use of the couch is not only a matter of personal preferences for many analysts, but its use is also a matter of considerable importance to the theory of technique.

## INTRODUCING THE USE OF THE COUCH

When an analytic patient either disallows or is anxious about going to the couch, or cannot because of excessive neurotic fear, much patience and understanding of the resistance is needed to alter or resolve the source of this particular interfering anxiety. Until then the treatment best proceeds in an upright sitting position.

It is quite understandable that any person would initially be hesitant before experiencing a procedure that seemed new and unfamiliar. At the outset it would appear to be of no advantage to the analysand to assume the recumbent position, and a suggestion to do this might meet with hesitation.

Although many analytic patients report an initial resistance to the use of the couch and object openly and strenuously, they later in the treatment usually acquiesce. Others express less obvious resistance and concern but proceed docilely to lie on the couch. Another group will only silently voice their objections to themselves. These latter persons may subsequently voice their preference to sit up and look at the analyst while talking. New patients coming for a first consultation often glance furtively and apprehensively at the couch as they sit down to commence their discussion of their problems. If they do not openly express themselves, they may inwardly voice the question, "Is he (or she) going to ask me to lie down on that?"

In addition to the supine position being unfamiliar as a mode of communication and therefore objectionable per se, this position often seems like a relationship where one person, the analyst, is in the superior position (sitting up) to the patient (lying down). It is understandable that most people question a relationship where one person is sitting up in what seems to be a superior position, while another lies down speaking to what often seems to be a blank wall. There is often quite a gap in time before the person in the recumbent position becomes aware of any benefits that may accrue to him as a result of his assuming the recumbent position. Furthermore, it often seems at first glance that removing someone from the viz-a-viz position discourages open communication. It would appear that recommending the couch is incongruous to progressive communication.

Having seen the couch ridiculed in cartoons, novels, or on television shows, many patients considering the use of the couch are often negatively suggestible. They resist seeing themselves identified with a role that is so commonly ridiculed. It is therefore quite understandable that many people are reluctant to accept a communication structure so out of keeping with the normal and which appears to have built into it a number of threatening elements.

The analyst too can be reluctant to assume a role in the chair behind the couch because he is also identified with a process that is so often publicly ridiculed. This reluctance can be reinforced by the skeptical and negative views and comments that many of his fellow professionals have regarding the use of the couch as an adjunct to treatment.

Because of various attitudes (conscious and unconscious) and beliefs on the part of both the patient and analyst, there can be considerable ambivalence in regard to the couch and when its use should be initiated. Consequently, there can be varying criteria and methods of introducing the patient to the use of the couch. Very often the criteria for when and how one should institute the use of the couch are influenced by the various cultural factors mentioned above, in addition to the analyst's own training and experiences.

In commencing the treatment, some therapists spend one or more sessions becoming acquainted with the patient's pathology and outlining the course of treatment they will follow. It is only after they have fixed this in their minds that they then invite the patient to lie down and "begin the analysis." Often in the introductory sessions the analyst will mention that the couch is to be used for the treatment and invite the patient's opinion about it. In those instances when the patient is a sophisticated person he or she has read about analysis or has had friends tell about it. Prior to starting treatment he has anticipated this invitation and taken it into consideration before making the decision to seek analytic treatment. He therefore is the least likely to raise any objection to the recumbent position. Some analysts invite their patients to lie on the couch in the very first session after it has been agreed that analysis will begin. Resistance analysis requires that any hesitation on the part of the patient be respected and explored. Some therapists will have their patients sit on the couch for a period of time, relax themselves, and try to become comfortable talking to their new therapist. It is after a period of time when the patient has gotten into the pattern of talking comfortably that he is invited to lie down. There are variations on this wherein the analyst may position himself during the initial sessions so that he can be seen from the couch and then some time afterward position himself behind the couch. Some psychoanalysts will only request that their patients lie on the couch if they are seen more than three or four times per week. Others, depending upon their orientation, will have their patients lie on the couch if they are seen once each week, or even every two weeks (Spotnitz, 1969). Some analysts will only selectively permit and encourage the use of the couch if the manifest psychopathology of the analysand falls into the catagory of one of the neuroses.

Braatøy (1954, p. 118) has said:

> Received by the friendly, interested analyst, the patient relaxes a bit in his chair. Giving, from this comfortable chair, information about himself and about experiences, acts, and conflicts which are painful, he perceives that the information does not call forth criticism or moral censure.
>
> On the background of this information, the therapist suggests a treatment which includes the couch.

Braatøy after making the analysand comfortable then proceeds to guide him to the couch. He explains to us his rationale for use of the couch and reveals the relationship between the relaxed recumbent position and the transference situation. It is against the backdrop of the relaxed posture the couch introduces that any displaced anxiety is made more apparent. He (p. 118) says

> In the supine position on the couch, the patient's muscles have little postural work to do. For this reason, the tension

they disclose is only determined by "psychological reasons," that is, by the patient's relation to the room including the person behind his back and by residual, chronic tensions in him. If the psychoanalyst in this situation continues to feed the patient with security, the tensions caused by the new, the actual situation will subside and the tensions determined by non-actual, internalized conflicts will be more clearly revealed. The clinician can then comment upon these tensions, which disclose themselves in movement or lack of movement, in typical or in highly individual postures. Expressed in psychoanalytic terminology, the analyst will then comment on "transference phenomena."

Another approach is utilized by Guntrip (1971, p. 184):

> I do not instruct a patient to lie on the couch. I wait to see what he will do, and when and why he wants to do something different.
>
> The whole matter was put to me quite clearly by one patient. He stood in the middle of the room and looked around, and then said, "I'll feel too grown up if I sit in that arm chair, but I'll feel too like a baby on that couch." In fact for a long time, he sat sideways on the couch. Then he sat up in the chair and his therapy became much more difficult and sticky. It was a defense, and he gave it up and went back on the couch. Then one session he put one leg up on the couch, and at the next session he put both legs up, and then when he really relaxed lying on the couch, accepting the dependent, helpless, anxious infant he actually felt himself to be, then things really began to move, and truly therapeutic results began to accrue.

Although Guntrip does not directly instruct his analysand to lie on the couch, the conflict enacted indicates an implied mandate to assume the supine position. This example illustrates the resistance to initially getting on the couch as also a defense against feeling dependent and helpless. The resolution of the defense becomes simultaneously a resolution of the resistance to the use of the couch.

Stein and Tarachow (1967, p. 485) make the following recommendations:

> The question of whether a patient should sit up facing the therapist or lie down on the couch is important here. Obviously, lying down on the couch has certain meanings to certain patients. Again, the decision will be based upon what is most useful to the patient, and a certain flexibility should be permitted to the patient, since with some patients, even those treated by psychoanalytic psychotherapy, it is easier for them to verbalize, particularly aggressive material, when they are not facing the therapist.

These authors reinforce a stand against a rigid view of the use of the couch. The idea of flexibility based on the quality of the analysands defenses is considered. This consideration should help arrive at an estimate of the timing and ultimate recommendation about lying on the couch.

Kelman and Vollmerhansen (1967, p. 413), followers of Karen Horney, also recommend a flexible attitude:

> This same flexibility obtains regarding "The Use of the Analytic Couch" (Kelman, 1954). He feels the issue is "What position and how moving from one physical position to another is better at a particular time for a particular patient to help move analysis forward more effectively?" Kelman also asked how can a patient be helped to avail himself effectively of physical mobility in the analytic situation and also how can this physical mobility be used to support and encourage all dimensions of mobility in patients for helping them toward self-realization. Because we see the analytic situation as a single integral reality, the preference and aversion for the couch and the vis-a-vis position of patients as well as of therapists with particular problems must be explored.
>     Our hope is that all patients will ultimately avail themselves of the couch in ways that it can be optimally used, for which no other position can be a substitute. We look to freer associating; more effective utilization of dreams, fantasies,

and slips; a regularity of the numbers and time of sessions, of arrangements for payment, and a diminuation or disappearance of absences and latenesses.

Phyllis Greenacre (1971, pp. 635–636) has spoken in considerable detail of the analytic setting, its meaning for both the analyst and analysand, the benefits of a flexible approach, and the distinction of what is said on and off the couch:

> No discussion of practical arrangements for psychoanalytic therapy would be complete without paying one's respects to the question of whether the couch or the chair is to be used by the analysand during his treatment session. Indeed, to many lay people, the use of the couch became the main or only index of whether the treatment was psychoanalytic or a discussion method. Couch meant psychoanalysis; chair meant no psychoanalysis. With the increased popularity of psychoanalysis, unfortunately some young psychiatrists became analysts through the purchase of a couch and the reading of the dream book; and with the increased interest in recent years in the hypnotic and drug and electroshock therapies, the couch is more or less routine equipment and no longer a mark of distinction. Although its use was probably originally derived from the hypnotic therapy with which analysis originated, it was retained—not as a residual organ —but because it was of service in inducing a state of mild relaxation and limiting gross movement in the analysand, a condition favorable for attention to the flow of associative thought so necessary for the exploration of unconscious connections. Furthermore, with the analyst sitting at the head of the couch, the patient is not distracted by watching the analyst's facial expression and attempting to read it and accommodate to it, while the analyst can rest his face the more by not having to be looked at all day long and to inhibit or control the unconscious blend of reaction and reflection in his facial expression. As every analyst knows, there are some patients in marginal relationship with reality who find it very difficult to talk unless communication is maintained through visual as well as through spoken contact. Such patients naturally require to be treated vis-a-vis, but generally require other marked changes in analytic technique as well.

Many analysts make a considerable distinction between what is said before the patient gets on the couch and immediately after he rises from it, from that which is couch born. Certainly there may be considerable significance in the difference in his postural relationship to the analyst and its connection with his utterances. One notices these things rather naturally with each patient and quite as naturally determines what importance to place upon them. Only a very compulsive analyst will want to determine an inexorable precision rule of interpretation about these matters or to prescribe every detail of the analyst's office. The general principle is to keep the physical arrangements of the office substantially the same throughout the treatment. Certainly this aids in limiting diverting influences and intrusions.

What Freud (1913b, p. 133–134) himself had to say on this subject deserves stating here:

> . . . On beginning the analytic treatment a word must be said about a certain ceremonial observance regarding the position in which the treatment is carried out. I adhere firmly to the plan of requiring the patient to recline upon a sofa, while one sits behind him out of sight. This arrangement has an historic meaning; it is the last vestige of the hypnotic method out of which psychoanalysis was evolved; but for many reasons it deserves to be retained. The first is a personal motive, one that others may share with me, however. I cannot bear to be gazed at for eight hours a day (or more). Since while I listen, I resign myself to the control of my unconscious thoughts. I do not wish my expression to give the patient indications which he may interpret or which may influence him in his communications. The patient usually regards being required to take up this position as a hardship and objects to it, especially when scoptophilia plays an important part in the neurosis. I persist in the measure, however, for the intention and the result of it are that all imperceptible influence on the patient's associations by the transference may be isolated and clearly outlined when it appears as a resistance. I know that many analysts work in a different way, though I do not know whether the main motive of their departure is the ambition to work in a different way or an advantage which they gain thereby.

Some analysts have interpreted Freud's words to mean that he forcefully urged his patients in the first session to lie on his couch. They have used these comments to reinforce a rigid view of the use of the couch. Actually Freud rather patiently encouraged the use of the couch and was content to analyze resistances to his recommendation. My own approach is to introduce the couch as early in the treatment as possible, but not if it might cause more than mild discomfort. Occasionally it is helpful to place a nervous patient on the couch for short intervals as a sample and introduction to its later use. Here is an example of this:

A businessman in his early forties came into treatment with the complaint of early morning terror coupled with feelings of helplessness and hopelessness and in moments of extreme distress would repeat the expression, "I want my mother." He sat upright facing me for many months. He had been in treatment previously with a number of other therapists and declined to use the couch because of his prior experience. He said that he experienced anxiety in lying on the couch. He again voiced his anxiety when I suggested once more that he might consider using the couch. He had been talking about his difficulty in sensing his feelings and I said he might be able to get these feelings while lying on the couch. In response to his mention of his apprehension, I told him he might rest on the couch until he became uncomfortable and then take his seat again. He agreed and got on the couch. After a few minutes he felt anxious, his breathing sounded more labored, and his body began to tense up. He remained on the couch for a total of about ten minutes, got up, and afterward felt immediately more comfortable. In the meantime it gave me an opportunity to get a number of impressions and form a series of hypotheses. It stimulated him to explore the sharp contrast in feelings before, during, and after being on the couch. They were feelings he continued to think about after his session.

In the next session he was in a much better mood. He had a few moments of anxiety in the morning, but they were of short duration, and in general he felt better. He explained that he realized that he had been operating on the principle that he should limit himself to his own area of direct business expertise. Actually, he said, he had a lot of interest in many businesses and had a wide range of competence. His father too had this range of abilities, but his mother because of her fears had held back the father. I told him that he seemed like the kind of person who may need to be engaged in a wide range of activities to operate at his best. He seemed pleased at this comment and related a number of business ventures he was considering. Then he mentioned that he often felt stir crazy if he stayed in his office more than a few hours. Why was this, he asked me. I asked him if he would be willing to lie on the couch while we explored this. He stated once again his apprehension about the couch, but proceeded to lie down. Again, on the couch he began to develop similar feelings of discomfort and asked me why this was happening. I began to tell him in detail my speculations that apparently he was excessively confined to his crib and to his playpen as a young child. I reflected back to him some of his numerous references to his mother as someone who held back, discouraged, or limited his assertiveness. He began to amplify about this. He talked about his feelings of spreading out and his fear of this. He began to recall many circumstances in his childhood and infancy. As he talked on the couch his labored breathing began to ease, his body began to relax, and his anxiety began to diminish. He found this to be a very helpful experience and was therefore able and interested in using the couch. For a long time he continued having the original symptoms connected with lying on the couch, but to a lesser degree. We were able to use these feelings to generate further understanding of his problems.

## RESISTANCE TO USING THE COUCH

Variations in techniques are a matter of the orientation of the therapist and his subjective opinion about his or her case. The question of resistance, however, is a matter of whether the patient fails to follow a procedure which the analyst thinks will be beneficial to the therapeutic process. Resistances are interferences to acting and talking in a way that lead the patient and the analyst to a complete understanding of the patient's emotional life so that he can become a fully healthy individual. There are some general rules which apply to the analysis of resistance. Resistances can not be subverted nor commanded out of the way but are to be explored and resolved. This means that each resistance must be investigated to discover its origin, its historical development, and its meaning to the life of the patient. When the resistance is explored and the feeling invested in it is released, the resistance thereby dissolves. This simultaneous analyzing and resolving of resistances is the means by which a treatment basis is established and is also the method whereby the patient may ultimately become cured of his emotional conflicts.

Hunt, Corman, and Ormont (1954, p. 99) have remarked about this process of resistance analysis as follows:

> Curiously enough, when the patient simply lies on the couch and tries to speak his thoughts he finds himself unable to speak easily and freely. He must constantly struggle with the impulse to hold back some idea or not talk at all, or to rearrange his words into pleasanter and more acceptable forms, so that the psychoanalyst has to work at ridding his patient of inhibitions which prevent or distort his free association, and no analysand associates in a completely free fashion until he is close to the end of treatment.

With certain patients, those who are of the narcissistic type and unresponsive to classical interpretation (Greenson, 1967), exploring the resistances is not always a helpful procedure. With such individuals investigation of their behavior can cause regression along with possible undesirable loss of ego functioning (Kohut, 1971). For them other resistance solvents may be more efficacious (Spotnitz, 1969).

An illustration of a type of resistance solvent advocated by Spotnitz was provided by a colleague (Mellinger, 1976). He writes:

I recall this example of using the feelings induced in me by a young woman (age 18) to resolve her resistance to lying on the couch. She had been insisting that she wanted me to like her, but that I really did not like her. She stated if I did like her I would be glad to have her sit up and face me and I would talk to her.

After much exploration of her resistance to lying on the couch I felt prepared for her next request for me to demonstrate that I liked her. When she made her complaint I told her, "I don't think you want me to like you, I think you want me to throw you out." "Why?" she exclaimed. I said, "Because when a patient wants me to like her, she follows the rule and lies on the couch and you don't want to do that." She almost ran to the couch saying, "Oh, if I knew that I would have gotten on the couch!" and she continued, "It's true. I think that I do want people to hate me." She then gave me an example of teasing her co-workers to get them to hate her. Now, months later, she continues to lie on the couch without any resistances other than verbal ones.

Where free association is the patient's task in the traditional process, the analyst's psychic posture, according to Freud's (1913) suggestion, should be one of the "free floating attention." A study of how this advice might be followed could lead to some useful observations relative to his use of the recumbent position in therapy.

By "free floating," Freud meant that the analyst's mind should be open not only to the verbal expressions of the patient but also open to those subtle thoughts, feelings, and fantasies which are induced by the analytic situation that might slip into his own mind. Equally, the analyst should be sufficiently open to those feelings and fantasies that are stimulated by his relationship with the patient and those feelings which intrude upon it. Hopefully, free-floating attention permits an open-minded, sensitive therapist to become aware of the thoughts and feelings induced by the patient in contrast with those independent of the patient and which are exclusive expressions of the analyst's own needs. This forms the basis for the analysis of counter-transference and counter-resistance phenomena. Reik (1948) has provided many illustrations of this. Also, the free-floating posture recommended by Freud helps provide the analyst with access to his own fantasy life. About this Greenson (1967, p. 401) has written:

> Just as the setting of the analytic situation promotes fantasy formation in the patient, it does so also in the analyst. His sitting behind the couch unseen, his abundant silence, the physical restrictions imposed on him, the emotional restraint, all tend to mobilize the analyst's imagination. Most important, however, is the fact that the patient's neurotic transference reactions cast the analyst in a variety of roles. He may become the dearly beloved or the hated enemy, the frightening father or the seductive mother in the patient's mind. It is the analyst's task to allow these developments to take place and to intervene only when it is helpful to the patient. More than that, it is his job to embellish and refine the character type the patient has displaced onto him, in order to gain a better understanding of its significance for the patient.

Roazen (1975, p. 123) commented on Freud's belief that the couch enlarged the scope of his therapeutic influence:

> Freud never altered his commitment to neutrality as the proper analytic approach. Thanks to the use of the couch, Freud felt, the patient does not have too much reality to cope with, and therefore encounters little interference in developing his fantasies about the analyst: hence a more efficient build-up of transference. The analyst's distance from his patients not only facilitates the analyst's rational insight, which might be impeded in a more commonplace setting, but also, Freud thought, expands the range of the kinds of patients accessible to analytic influence. Freud (1919) wrote "I had nothing in common—neither race, education, social position nor outlook upon life in general without affecting their individuality" [p. 162].

Benedek (1953) has suggested that the analyst needs to be screened in order to deal with his own emotions in relative privacy, that is, to recognize his counter-transference and then to manage his feelings.

In examining the analyst's attitude Roazen (1975, pp. 123–124) has this to say:

> If an analyst is afraid that patients will find weak spots and feels that inspection is a hostile act, then there would of course be a strain involved in face-to-face therapy. The use of a couch can also help the analyst avoid emotional intimacy with patients. With certain kinds of patients, who may—for a variety of reasons—be frightened of lying down, a modern analyst would have to contravene Freud's recommendation and permit the patient to sit up. But none of the limitations of the couch should obscure the general point that it may still be the easiest method of allowing the patient to relax and free-associate. The impersonality of the analyst can ease the way to the patient's most private and personal self-disclosures.

Although some critics consider Freud's aversion to being looked at as a personal and neurotic idiosyncracy, many contemporary analysts agree with Chessick (1971, p. 308) whose experience seems to vindicate Freud's preference:

> There was no doubt in my mind that having at least some of my patients on the couch during full days of outpatient psychotherapy did make a difference in terms of my own comfort and ability to concentrate. No matter how relaxed we are with our patients, they often will not let us forget our personal facial expressions, body postures, and quirks, and even though we are comfortable with ourselves it is ridiculous to argue that being stared at all day does not produce an instinctive guarding response that definitely does take energy and impair concentration. Whether greater relaxation on the part of the therapist was the factor or whether the magical factor of the couch was involved, several patients did remarkably better in psychotherapy when they were placed on the couch.

Granted that the free-floating emotional posture on the part of the analyst is beneficial to the analysis, how, we may ask, is the physical setting of the analytic situation relevant to this posture in one way or another? There are any number of possible answers to this question. For example, it might be maintained that a well-disciplined therapist should simultaneously be able to face another person, listen to him, observe him, think about what he is asking, talk to him, and also be aware of the workings of his own psyche. Such an assertion could be challenged. The upright face-to-face arrangement is very difficult, day in and day out, especially if it must be maintained for six to eight hours per day. With increasing experience and improved ability to focus on one's own thoughts and on the patient's deeper thoughts and feelings, analysis becomes more fatiguing. Psychoanalysis is hard work. It is productive for the analyst and patient to cooperate and try to arrange a setting to do this work in as efficient and relaxed a manner as possible.

Freud found, as has almost every psychoanalyst since, that he functioned better at his work when he was not obliged to face his patients. The analyst usually finds that in approaching his task in a relaxed way, sitting in a chair designed to provide him with the maximum in comfort, with his ear attuned to the other person's communications, without concern about looking or not looking or being looked at, he functions better. Hollander (1965, p. 102) has stated, "It is difficult to be under close scrutiny hour after hour. Not only does sitting behind the couch make it possible to be less concerned about facial expressions, but also to be more relaxed in posture."

There are other ways that the patient's use of the recumbent position can ease the tensions of the analyst and contribute to the development of positive counter-transference attitudes, particularly in potentially difficult, impulse-ridden people whose inclination is to put their thoughts and feelings into actions which threaten the treatment situation. Spotnitz (1969, p. 170) has framed this situation as follows:

> But any anxieties that the patient may act destructively under the sway of his emotions are dissipated later in treatment when he lies on the couch in a relaxed way and is able to maintain that posture no matter what he feels. The analyst then experiences a strong sense of security and control. He feels more and more at ease with the patient, more and more interested in helping him understand what has been going on in their relationship. The patient's growing desire for information about his functioning dovetails with the analyst's lively interest in providing it. He becomes aware of admiration and genuine affection for the patient, and at times of strong desire either to "mother" or "father" him, perhaps both.

On this assumption, when the patient lies on the couch and the analyst sits in a comfortable way which enables him to function at a maximum level of his ability, the analysis goes best; it follows that anything less than this optimal situation is a resistance. As a resistance it requires investigation at some point in the treatment. It should be emphasized, however, that the resistance here has not to do with the question of lying on the couch or with the analyst's not adequately relaxing. It is a resistance against the cooperation needed between patient and therapist in order to work through any treatment to a healthy conclusion.

It is not advisable that a patient be compelled to lie on the couch under any kind of threat. Its use should always be an expression of either his own interest in doing so or of his willingness to cooperate with what he perceives is the analyst's belief that it will make the analysis go better.

In terms of cooperation Greenson (1967, pp. 214–215) includes the following caveat about the "working alliance":

We cannot repeatedly demean a patient by imposing rules and regulations upon him without explanation and then expect him to work with us as an adult. If we treat him as a child by behaving with imperious and arbitrary attitudes and expectations, he will remain fixated to some form of infantile neurotic transference reaction. For a working alliance it is imperative that the analyst show consistent concern for the rights of the patient throughout the course of the analysis. This means that we indicate our concern not only for the neurotic misery the patient brought into the analysis and suffers outside of the analysis, but also for the pain that the analytic situation imposes on him. Aloofness, authoritarianism, coldness, extravagance, complacency, and rigidity do not belong in the analytic situation. Let me illustrate with some typical examples.

All new or strange procedures are explained to the patient. I always explain to the patient why we ask him to try to associate freely and why we prefer to use the couch. I wait for the patient's questions or responses before I suggest that he try the couch. All my utterances to the patient are spoken with a tone of voice which indicates my awareness and my respect for the patient's predicament. I do not talk down to the patient, but I make sure he understands my ideas and my intention. I use ordinary language, avoiding technical terms and intellectualized modes of speech. I treat him as an adult whose cooperation I need and who will soon be experiencing analytic material.

Based upon this flexible approach, there need to be no fixed numbers of sessions before lying on the couch, whether it be the first, second, or fifth. What matters more is the analysis of any fears, beliefs, or wishes that inhibit the analysis in this posture. Ultimately, this analysis of resistance becomes more important than any aspect of the physical setting.

More often than not, people object to lying on the couch at first. An example of this is a patient who said with annoyance, "I would prefer to sit up and talk to you." "How come?" she was asked. She replied, "When I talk without looking at you I feel like I am talking to the walls and no one is listening to me."

The history of this resistance was that in her childhood her mother often severely reprimanded her for not listening and for not paying attention. This criticism was repeated in school by a number of teachers. She identified with her mother/teachers and was inclined to the view the analyst as her inattentive child/student. Often, to parents, being listened to means being obeyed.

Another patient was much more strenuous in his objections to lying down. They were approximately as follows: "It is like surrendering." "It would be an act of subordination." "I have too much pride." "I would feel stupid." "It would bother me not being able to see you." "I would consider it an intrusion on my privacy." "My doing it would remove an aspect of equality between us." "It's too much like the posture of sleep and sex."

All of these objections were equivalents of attitudes toward the analyst and the therapy and as such were resistances to be investigated. Eventually when these resistances were systematically explored and understood the objections disappeared.

There is another aspect to the manifestation of resistances. That is, acting out certain neurotic patterns and character traits is frequently a substitute for talking. This pertains not only to the patient but also in many instances to the therapist. Spotnitz (1969, p. 101) has called attention to negative or discomforting feelings the analyst can develop which the patient can perceive and which can interfere with the use of the couch. He says:

> . . . a refusal to assume it (the couch position), or to remain on the couch throughout the session, cannot always be attributed exclusively to the patient's uncooperative attitude. Resistance to use of the couch is frequently reinforced by the patient's perception that the therapist is uneasy about his being there.

Greenson (1967, p. 400) has pointed out that the analyst can possess traits which can compulsively urge him
arbitrarily to use or not use the couch as a manifestation of
certain character traits. He writes:

> I am impressed by the high percentage of psychoanalysts
> who suffer from a marked degree of stage fright. It is so
> striking that I am forced to assume that one of the motives
> that makes psychoanalysis attractive as a profession is the
> analyst's hidden position behind the couch. The important
> instrumentality of facilitating the transference neurosis by
> restraining one's emotional responses and keeping oneself
> relatively anonymous may well be touching on this patho-
> logical source. Modesty and a sense of privacy are the analo-
> gous healthy traits of character which might impel one to
> find this aspect of psychoanalytic technique attractive.
>     The decisive factor is how fixed, rigid, and intense is the
> shyness of the analyst. As long as he has some flexibility and
> can overcome his timidity when it is necessary it may not
> become a serious hindrance. On the other hand, strong
> unexpressed exhibitionistic impulses in an analyst can
> become a problem in the other direction. For such analysts
> the position behind the couch and blanketing of their emo-
> tional responses may become a chronic frustration, which
> may lead to eruptions of inconsistant behavior or uncon-
> scious provocation of acting out in the patient.

The character traits of narcissism and exhibitionism
will continually seek expression. The use of the couch
tends to frustrate these drives, both in the patient and
in the analyst. The patient on the couch, unsure as to
whether he is receiving the attention he requires, will react both with anxiety and anger at the deprivation of an
audience.

A woman who finally consented to use the couch after
many months of treatment would writhe and fidget while
lying there. She mentioned her husbands criticism of her
attire and her careless way of sitting and lying around the
house in front of the children. She admitted liking to "pa-

rade around" even if it bothered some people. She would inevitably wear tight, short, low-cut dresses which her wriggling on the couch would shorten even more. It was not until she complained of her compulsive rummaging in her husbands affairs—"acting like a detective"—that a connection was made between her compulsive need to see and her libidinal wish to be seen even though it caused others discomfort.

These traits are not always limited to the patient. The therapist who has this need to be seen will usually find some reason for not letting himself out of his patient's sight. If the couch is ever used, it is soon given up. Some therapists have certain thespian needs that receive gratification through performing. It is interesting to observe students in training describe their work in both individual psychoanalytic work and in group psychotherapy. Certain students show obvious pleasure in their work with groups which allows more latitude of expression for the therapist and greater appreciation from the therapeutic audience. They describe their sessions with individual patients in a heavy phlegmatic manner while discussions of group sessions are sparkled by smiles and chuckles.

The above traits act as a resistance to the therapy only insofar as they are extensively acted upon rather than ultimately diverted into analytic talking. Any activity in the session that is engaged in rather than talked about is acting out and therefore a resistance. A common one is for the person on the couch to jump and say, "I've got to go to the bathroom!" Another is to suddenly sit up and look at the analyst or to continue talking on the same subject but now sitting up. Both are examples of acting out. In the first, the patient failed to describe the build-up of feelings, possibly a reaction to the thoughts he was expressing. Therefore, he was acting rather than talking. In the second example, the patient sat up without giving expression to the feelings that led to this change of posture, thereby avoiding talking about the wishes or needs giving rise to this action. What he was talking about was not related directly or strongly to the more dominant thought and feeling that led him to sit up. The more dominant theme was therefore circumvented by the action. This by-passing of the verbal expression of thoughts and feelings should be discouraged. One way is to educate the patient to request permission before rising from the couch in order to give the analyst an opportunity to further explore what is happening.

In terms of resistance strategy, when the patient finds it difficult to stay on the couch because of poor impulse control or negative suggestibility, special and nontraditional interventions may be used. Spotnitz (1969, pp. 89, 198) has suggested the following:

> The practioner may prohibit one or another pattern of behavior in the sessions, such as getting off the couch or smoking, as a matter of therapeutic strategy.

> A person who says he can no longer lie on the couch may be told, "It's about time you found the couch intolerable and wanted to leave it."

There are a number of interventions that an analyst can make to discourage the patient from leaping off the couch unexpectedly. One is to ask at the beginning of the session what the analyst does to create a feeling of wanting to sit up, and then exploring why that feeling is aroused. The patient is asked what would happen if the wish to sit up is ignored. The more extensive such a discussion is, the greater the ego strength to resist the impulse.

Another strategy is to request an impulsive patient to sit up for about 5 or 10 minutes at the start of the session, then rise about 5 or 10 minutes before the end. Most people become curious at such a request and when it is explained that they are being helped to tolerate their limited capacity to lie on the couch, they often become more willing to tolerate the supine position.

A final comment regarding the use of the couch in this

regard has to do with a form of protocol. For those therapists who take seriously the use of the couch the behavior
of the analyst toward the patient before and after the couch
is utilized is quite formalized in the sense that the analyst
behaves differently in each instance. The patient learns that
no matter what is communicated on the couch, the analyst
will attempt to receive and part with him or her in a friendly
and courteous fashion. On arriving for an appointment the
patient should be greeted in a mildly positive manner with
the analyst behaving like a good host or hostess intending
to make a guest as comfortable as possible. The author is
usually standing and attentive to an arriving patient. Sometimes inquiries are made, if there seems to be a comment
needed, as to whether the room is warm or cool enough.
If the patient feels cool a blanket may be provided.

Once on the couch, this distinction is put aside and the
patient is responded to strictly in terms of the kinds of
therapeutic strategies that will facilitate the treatment. In
the extreme, the patient may be told very unpleasant and
uncomplimentary things about him or herself. There may
be an exchange of very heated or even abusive words as
sometimes occurs. The patient may shout or cry, feel em-
barrassed, or terrified, but when the end of the hour ar-
rives, there is, so to speak, a truce, and the parting occurs
in as friendly, if not neutral a manner as possible. This
"island" of regression that is confined to the use of the
couch in the long run acts as a lubricant to the analytic
process.

## GEOGRAPHY OF THE ANALYTIC SETTING

With regard to the physical elements of the treatment, two
further important aspects may be examined; the position of
the analyst's chair relative to the couch and the posture of
the person lying upon the couch.

The way that a patient lies on the couch is very informative. Whether the legs are crossed, straight, or taut; whether the hands are behind the head or folded on the stomach, all communicate vital information. The analyst's observation and understanding of this can permit him to comprehend the nonverbal, frequently unconscious information given by body posture, movements, or lack of movement on the couch.

Two illustrations are offered of how physical posturing can communicate emotional needs. One patient on the couch would compulsively turn his head around to look at the analyst every few minutes. He did this for almost a year. No suggestion or assurance could deter this behavior. He would suddenly become extremely anxious and had to convince himself that the analyst had not left, that he was still there by looking directly at him. After a while the analyst could predict when the patient would turn about by the developing tautness in his body. While very young the patient suffered a period of very long absence from his family and had to overcome his fear of abandonment.

A woman writhed on the couch. She ultimately came to understand her simultaneous fear of rape and wish for physical intimacy from her analyst. Her writhing was an anticipatory expression of this fear and wish.

In addition to what the patient does on the couch, how and where the analyst sits in order to observe the person on the couch is important. For example, to be seated directly behind the patient, and particularly to the rear and at right angles to the couch, may obscure much of what physically transpires upon it. Although the patient may not be able to see the therapist, it is usually important that the therapist have the opportunity to see the patient. A seating arrangement having the chair to the left or right of the couch, permitting full view, is therefore favorable.

In speaking of positioning Rosenbaum (1967, p. 186) says of the opportunities to observe the patient's gestures and facial expression:

> My own experiences have confirmed this possibility in a great many instances, where ample opportunities have presented themselves for making exactly such observations. However, there have been many occasions when my view of the patient was partially or totally obstructed, permitting only the observation of postural involvement. This leaves me to assume that some revealing and important facial expressions must have escaped detection on my part. Despite the probability that the couch position does not afford the analyst with constant control over the direct observation of a patient, in most cases it will provide him with ample opportunity to do so to a considerable extent: In my own experience I have never been confronted with a significant hide-and-seek problem in my efforts at observation during the course of a psychoanalysis. However, it is conceivable that it may present a problem here and there, at which time only it may require special attention or modification.

Braatøy (1954, p. 154) emphasizes the need to insure maximum visual observation of the patient. He says,

> Formalized in psychoanalytic technique, this attitude has focused psychoanalyst's attention of the patient's words or lack of words. It has made them into listeners—not observers. My analyst, Otto Fenichel, sat in a low chair behind the head of the couch where he could not see my face. When I questioned him about this, he argued that he was so trained in listening to patients that, by their words, their way of speaking or of not speaking, he could accurately gauge the emotional tension in them. Admitting that the experienced psychoanalyst may be able to do so to a great extent, one, nevertheless, is a bit surprised that we, in our very difficult work, should deprive ourselves of the steady flow of information about the patient's emotional tension, his affect or blocking of affect, which we get by directly observing his face, respiration, and movements on the couch.

He says further that for some therapists, contrary to being a restraint, the chair behind the couch can be perceived as part of their pension plan. Braatøy (p. 116) writes:

> Some overworked, aging analysts feel the deep chair behind the patient's couch not as a prison but as a position where at last they can whisper to their deceased mothers the famous epitaph: "Now you have peace—and so have I." If one asks such a person to change, to look in addition to listening, to rearrange the situation if need be, one may provoke intense irritation.

Braatøy, who was strongly influenced by Wilhelm Reich, may be placing undue emphasis on the visual elements of the treatment. It is not that these elements are unimportant, but usually the patient's physical presentation on arrival and departure and his deviation from a norm of behavior we come to expect of him, is more than sufficient for the information we require to successfully carry out the treatment.

Another factor in considering the use of the couch is the setting of the office in which the patient finds himself. Kelman (1954) writes in considerable detail about the physical arrangement of the entire office and the importance of the visual image greeting the arriving patient. He describes the states he and a patient experience as they move from certain chairs in the office to the couch. In his view the gestalt of the office setting has great significance for the patient.

In my opinion the physical layout of the analyst's office has importance mainly in the initial interview. Once the treatment has commenced the patient becomes accustomed to the office setting and comes to expect whatever he was first introduced to in the treatment. The office setting is often considered by the analysand as an extension of the analyst's personality. Many people have commented on various objects in my office and asked if I recently acquired them. They are usually surprised to learn that these objects were here but apparently unnoticed by them during their first interviews with me. As the transference resistance is resolved, they become more aware of me and my office.

A final comment about the construction and form of the couch, which is a matter of some variability, may be helpful here. The first couch used in psychoanalysis, that of Freud, was actually a rather common cloth-covered sofa used in that Victorian era during the development of this new therapy. Subsequently the most popular form of couch to be used by analysts is the green or black leather-covered divan. There are practical reasons for this more stringent form for the couch. As any novice soon learns, a cloth-covered couch put to constant use can be in tatters in a few years. The leather or vinyl covered divan is much longer lasting and easier to keep clean. It furthermore announces itself as distinctive, functional, and specifically oriented to the professional activities of the analyst.

My own view is that the couch should be both functional and comfortable. To this end I have added a soft washable rug and a pillow on my couch. The choice of a couch in the consulting room is more likely to be a matter of the analysts preference than any specific technical advantage.

## APPLICABILITY TO DIFFERENT AGE GROUPS AND DISORDERS

The ongoing controversy over the use of the couch in the treatment of children, adolescents, and psychotics, indicates it to be influential for the treatment in one way or another (Gordon, *et al.,* 1967). Most therapists seem to hold that such patients are most successfully treated in an upright position and claim that the recumbent position can even be harmful.

In general, Frieda Fromm-Reichmann (1959) is

against the use of the couch. She is quite emphatic in opposing its use for regressed patients. She says, "the couch regulation is neither understood nor followed by the psychotic patient."

On the other hand, one analyst, Spotnitz (1969), states that he uses the couch with patients of any age or disturbance, unless it poses too much distress upon a particular patient. He believes that when the therapist cannot work with a patient on the couch it is usually a problem of counter-transference. When the schizophrenic patient lacks the needed tolerance to recline on the couch, Spotnitz (1969) utilizes the patient's family to educate the patient. He (pp. 78, 183) writes:

> Recently I have been enlisting the aid of a responsible member of the patient's family in training him, either before entering treatment or in its rudimentary stage, to lie down and talk for 50 minutes at home. The relative is instructed to listen attentively while the patient talks, and just interpose a brief question or two about external realities when he is silent. This supplementary procedure, I find, makes it easier for some patients with severe disturbances to be treated on the analytic couch.

> "Lie on the couch and talk" is a typical reformulation of the fundamental rule for the schizophrenic patient.

Boyer (1966), in an article on the office treatment of psychotics, also claims good results using the couch with his patients.

Haak (1957) worries about the dangers connected with "too deep" a regression on the couch. He insists that a patient sit up "when the patient's ego was about to lose control completely and be submerged with chaotic and unruly id-impulses." Haak reports three cases where he insisted the patients sit up, and other "borderline" cases, where a marked and striking change occurred when the patient switched to face-to-face position. This one patient became "entirely reasonable" and "no longer the trou-

blesome child that I just before with much difficulty tried
to help."

Neither Anna Freud (1946a) nor Melanie Klein (1954)
recommend the supine position in the treatment of children. While Klein's play therapy seems to preclude the use
of the couch for the smaller child, even with the older
adolescent her active interpretive method seems to be
based more on a vis-a-vis encounter than the passive analytic approach more suited to the couch.

A colleague (Junge, 1976) related that a five-year-old
girl she was treating questioned her regarding the purpose
of a cradle standing upright in the consulting room. On
having it explained that it was for small children to lie in,
the little girl exclaimed, "I want to lie in it." The girl proceeded to lie in the cradle during that session and many
that followed and talked very comfortably to her analyst in
a very meaningful way. The analyst was both surprised and
pleased by the positive results in the treatment.

In discussing the obsessional patient Caligor and Wittenberg (1967) argue against the traditional psychoanalytic
position and discourage the use of the couch. They (p. 431)
maintain:

> The use of the couch is definitely not necessary, nor is it
> probably indicated with a truly obessional person. Use of the
> couch tends to increase the depth of the patient's dimin-
> ished self-esteem and to encourage regression, frequently a
> risky therapeutic procedure with an obsessional. Also, the
> silence evoked by the couch tends to encourage anxiety, and
> certainly these people have too much anxiety. Though si-
> lence and a hovering kind of attention is not enough for the
> obsessional, an attitude of friendliness or benevolence is
> equally inappropriate. Rather a degree of formality, of dis-
> tance, and of directness is indicated.

Saul (1958) states that the schizoid may need all possible help in discriminating his own fantasies and images of
childhood and the current real relationship to the analyst.

He needs help in strenthening his grasp of reality at the expense of his fantasizing and in tolerating and resolving rather than intensifying the transference. The analyst must evaluate in each patient what may be gained in freer fantasy by using the couch. By permitting temporarily the attenuation of the ego's grasp of reality, the analyst may enhance the patient's ability to make use of the analytic experience in his real life.

Speaking of this need to apply a sophisticated understanding of the case in order to decide whether the use of the couch may be applicable and helpful, Chessick (1971, pp. 312–13) remarks:

> Each case must be decided on its own merit, depending on the aims of the treatment, the psychodynamics of the patient, and the particular phase or problems that are at hand. The therapist must try to determine how the patient deals with affect hunger when it is stirred up. He must look for signs of paranoid thinking or depression, as well as for signs of dangerous acting out such as speeding while driving an automobile or drug taking. He must judge the importance of visual contact, the role of introjection of the therapist through the eyes, and the need to defend against such wishes. Then he must decide if the face-to-face or the couch position is more desirable, and he must be willing to switch as needed.

Chessick (p. 313) says further:

> It is obvious that beginners should not attempt to place borderline patients on the couch. The couch is a sophisticated tool in psychotherapy, a tool which, like obstetrical forceps depends on the skill and experience of the man who uses it.

This evaluation is difficult to make. Occasionally the patterns of expected convention obscure the best direction for treatment. A number of personal experiences have helped the author better discern this path.

Early in my clinical training I had several experiences concerning the use of the couch that left me with vivid impressions. It was the policy of the clinic in which I worked to screen all patients applying for treatment in order to determine what type of therapy would be best for them. If they suffered mild disorders, that is, neurotic disturbances, and could come frequently, they were referred to students who would treat them psychoanalytically under supervision. If the patient could not come frequently, psychoanalytic supportive therapy would be the recommended treatment. If the patients were more disturbed, that is, depressed, borderline, or schizophrenic, an eclectic or psychoanalytic psychotherapy was in order, and sessions would be limited to one or at most two visits per week.

There were a number of unwritten guidelines that applied to these various treatments. If the patient was neurotic and was in therapy three or more times per week, the treatment would be considered psychoanalysis (applying of course the basic consideration of resistance and transference analysis) and the use of the couch would be considered an inherent part of the therapy. If the patients were more disturbed and seen less frequently than three times each week, the use of the couch was ruled out.

The reasoning for this was that because the couch induced regression in people this was to be avoided in those who could not be seen frequently and supported. Especially for those more disturbed individuals, for example, depressives or schizophrenics, whose egos were fragile and whose defenses were primitive, the regression which the couch would foster was to be avoided.

One of the first patients assigned to me was Miss A, a very attractive 22-year old woman. The interviewing psychiatrist diagnosed her as paranoid schizophrenic and suggested she be given supportive therapy once per week. My first year of Miss A's treatment went rather badly. She was a very unhappy woman who sat mutely opposite me with her head averted to the side, or else she stared at the floor. I had a very difficult time during this first year getting her to do any talking. Bit by bit I pieced together her emotional story:

Miss A's father had died when she was young and after emotionally using her to replace the dead husband, the mother placed her in a Catholic boarding school. At about the age of 13 something occurred which was very distressing. One day as she was walking, Miss A noticed that wherever she looked thick twigs and pieces of wood appeared to her as though they were penises. This became increasingly upsetting until finally one day she disclosed her problem to the priest in confession. The response she got from the priest was unexpected. He severely rebuked her for seeing these terrible things, shouted at her, and told her that she must stop this disgusting behavior. Miss A was very frightened.

Not long after this, the illusion of seeing penises everywhere stopped and in its place, without her awareness of the transition, came an illusion that was worse than the original one. She now had the unshakeable belief that mounted on the front of her face was a monstrous nose. No amount of persuasion could convince her that her nose was other than large and ugly. This was why she had no friends, no men interested in her, why the women where she worked would not talk to her, and why she had to walk with her face averted or looking down, or covered by a newspaper or magazine. It was also why she was convinced I held her in disgust and would want nothing to do with someone as repulsive as she.

Although this information gave much to think about, it was of little help in resolving my frustration with a treatment situation that was so stalemated. One day, after about a year of therapy an idea occurred to me, and I inquired of Miss A whether I reminded her of the priest who had so upset her in confession. After thinking of this awhile, she said yes. I looked like him, sat like him, and glanced at her like he did. After reflecting about this awhile, I asked her if it would be helpful to lie on the couch. She said yes with more enthusiasm than I had ever heard from her.

The change in her was extremely surprising to me. She no longer felt I was staring at her, and she was able to talk to me much more freely. Instead of silent sessions, we had relatively active conversations. Gradually she lost her pre-occupation with her nose and began dating a young man whom she eventually married.

There was a serious mishap shortly after Miss A began to lie on the couch. One of the other students seeking an empty room accidently opened the door to my office and observed Miss A on the couch. He apparently reported this to the clinic director because a few days later I was asked to come in for a conference. I was severely reprimanded for putting a psychotic patient on the couch and was given no chance to explain my reasons. My final solution to this dilemma was to lock the door whenever I was in session with her.

Shortly after I placed Miss A on the couch I was assigned to another patient, Mrs. B. Mrs. B was then about 48 years of age, very thin, divorced, unemployed, and on high doses of tranquillizers. She was diagnosed as paranoid schizophrenic, had had 35 electroshocks administered, had spent four years in a state hospital, and was very frail and frightened when I began to treat her. Her sickness had begun with very real terrifying hallucinations. She has attempted to work a number of times but had been unable to do so because of her fears, her self-consciousness, and the crippling effects of the high doses of tranquillizers.

Mrs. B also had trouble talking to me. She had much anxiety and would constantly repeat her fear and wish not to have to return to the state hospital. Becoming increasingly frustrated and aware of my success with Miss A on the couch, I suggested to Mrs. B that she lie on the couch. She did so quite willingly and seemed cheered by the idea that since I had recommended the couch, I was going to analyze her. She figured that since I was going to analyze her, she was not as hopeless as she had concluded.

Being a very sophisticated and highly intelligent person, Mrs. B knew that analytic patients are supposed to "free-associate," and she commenced to do so. I then began to hear the fascinating story of her life interspersed with anecdotes, dreams, thoughts, and feelings. Instead of decompensating, as I had been warned people like Mrs. B tend to do, she began to rapidly improve. Within a year she had regained her former teaching position and within two years she was appointed an associate professor at one of the nearby colleges. Mrs. B subsequently remarried and now about 15 years later continues to do well.

Another patient, Miss C, who suffered from neurotic hysteria, found it impossible to lie on the couch at the inception of therapy. She experienced an overwhelming amount of anxiety and had to be treated sitting up until it was learned that her mother had indoctrinated her in early childhood to believe that men would hurt her. This idea leading to a fear of rape had become a profound unconscious source of anxiety. Making it conscious and working it through permitted her to be able to relax on the couch.

A patient whom I treated successfully had early in the therapy displayed elements of psychosis and severe depression. She had made a number of suicide attempts. Later on a prominent neurologist diagnosed her condition as a disorder of the temporal lobe. Toward the end of the treatment I asked her why she had not manifested these psychotic-like seizures in my office. She said it was because of the couch. The induced relaxing feelings and the security of the couch helped her to maintain her control.

I am thankful to a colleague (Smith, 1975) for a vignette of treatment on the couch of a ex-hospitalized paranoid schizophrenic patient.

On Tuesday, December 16, 7 P.M., Miss E bombarded me with explosions of hostile transference feelings. She lay down on the couch and continued: "My feelings are unimportant. Only yours count. You don't support anything I say. You never listen to me. I feel very manipulated here. You have a way of negating anything I feel. You turned the page just when I expressed my feelings, and I interpret that as rejecting something and making me more aware of the fact that I just expressed a feeling. I never saw anything like it. I don't know what you are putting in the air for me to feel so angry. It must be thoughts I am having that I am not expressing that are making me very angry." With that statement began an improvement in thinking that was incredible. Excuse the word, but it truly seemed magical.

Shortly after this she said to me in a very low and threatening tone, "You be very careful this session. You be very careful what you say. You make me feel hatred for you and the more I lay here the angrier I get." Her throat began to itch. She asked the reason. This time when I asked for speculations I got them: "Unless it's a reaction to me expressing something, or that it wants to express more." She diverted for a few seconds and then, "I wanted a reason why this area was itching me so much." I answered, "Your speculation was a very good one." And then I understood another facet of the narcissistic process for she said, "I have already forgotten what I have figured out myself. I have already forgotten what I came up with myself. I have already negated what I thought myself. To identify yourself with even your own creative thinking is to feel the anxiety of separation."

Miss E's reference to the couch went as follows: "I did notice, it seemed as though there is an impression of me lying here right now. It seemed like I was concentrating on lying here rather than getting into feelings with you. I really . . . Well my body feels very still, and I feel most of my weight very much planted down on the couch, and I have not really let myself be that much a part of the couch which makes me feel like there is a certain amount of resistance I was giving into, giving up. I think that I . . . My mother telling me my father won't support this treatment any more after the end of December makes me appreciate it more." Upon rereading the above I am struck by these words: impression, planted, resistance, support. Miss E used the word "impression" in the sense she was being acted upon. The prone position kept her from getting into me. She says she felt planted on the couch and she felt a part of it. The couch afforded her some kind of mergable sustenance. The couch offers her a kind of narcissistic attachment which allows her to give up a certain amount of resistance. The couch is a transitional object. She speaks of not having support to continue therapy, but the couch offered physical support to her body and apparently to her thoughts as well. A kind of support she states neither her mother nor I provide. It leads me to speculate about the physical handling she had as an infant. The words above deal with many early sensations of feelings of inside and outside, of what's pressing in, holding up, of her own weight being a part of, or needing support, or pressing down on, or into someone or thing.

Braatøy (1954, p. 287) cautions against any reckless tampering with defenses that the couch can potentially loosen:

> If we then connect the patient's defensive attitude toward the couch and toward free associations (his "resistance") with the possibility of something resembling a latent psychosis, the contradictions in the patient's attitude to therapy become meaningful. Behind the rigid (correct) surface he has the terrified child's need for help. At the same time he strains against a technique which by trying to dissolve some of his defenses may let loose forces which he has conscious and unconscious reasons for being afraid of. He wants therapy for very good reasons; he may for just as good reasons be afraid of a treatment which aims at dissolving, disclosing, and analyzing in order to release and find out.

He (p. 290) says further:

> A latent psychotic or a psychotic in a face-to-face setting cooperates much better and may be without the hesitancy and the shyness of the neurotic. He blocks, becomes suspicious and resists therapy, if on the couch. He may block to such an extent that the classic psychoanalytic frame appears as the obstacle to treatment. If a therapist mainly influenced

by such experiences advocates the face-to-face setting in all cases, he neglects or has forgotten that the couch and recumbent position can be an important means in bringing out tensions and in changing the set-up from pleasant conversation to something concerned with (unconscious) tensions in the patient.

In distinguishing the differences between psychoanalysis and psychotherapy, Blanck and Blanck (1974, p. 129, 130) believed that even if the treatment is not psychoanalysis, the use of the couch is not necessarily contraindicated. They say:

> There is no contraindication to the use of the couch in psychotherapy if its purpose is clear. For some psychotherapy patients regression and fantasizing are undesirable, and if patients are found to be subject to these on the couch, they are better treated sitting up. Depending on the nature of the case, some patients also need to see the therapist to know he is there. For others, it is more desirable to learn that the object exists even if he is not in sight.
>
> We do not recommend the overanxious procedure in which the patient is asked to sit up the moment his productions on the couch begin to sound psychotic-like to the therapist. There is no magic cure for psychosis in the simple process of sitting up. Ego-building work can be done in the recumbent position, if that is where the patient happens to be, and it can be more alarming than reassuring to him to be commanded to sit up. If the therapist finds that he regresses too much and that primary process predominates, he can introduce reality while the patient is in any other position. While we ourselves prefer to have our psychotherapy patients sit, especially if object relations are blurred, some of them prefer to lie down and there is usually no reason to deprive them of this status symbol. The psychoanalytically sophisticated patient, in particular, is likely to think that he is psychotic unless he is lying down. Rather than debate the diagnosis with him, we allow him the couch.
>
> There are many patients who fear the couch. They are defending against powerful symbiotic wishes, loss of identity

and of regression, which may not be reversible. Such patients should not be forced to lie down. Often they choose to do so after their symbiotic fears are understood as wishes and are no longer projected upon the therapist as his need to envelop. On his part, of course, the therapist has to be very certain that his regard for the patient's autonomy and ego growth is such that he will usually not gratify these symbiotic longings, although it is his task to interpret them.

In speaking of the problem of evaluation of the applicability of the couch to various diagnostic categories of patients, Chessick (1971, p. 313) places the principal emphasis on the skill of the therapist. He says:

> It is not the couch, it is the man who uses it that counts. When the therapist possesses the proper training and experience, the couch can become a useful tool in the treatment of some borderline patients in certain phases or situations in their treatment. This demands good training, experience, alertness to the material, self-understanding on the part of the therapist, and a constant assessment of the anxiety levels of both the patient and the therapist. Generalizations about use and non-use of couch completely miss the point, which is that anyone who undertakes the psychotherapy of borderline patients must demand the highest standards of training and self-understanding from himself or he runs the same risks as the inexperienced surgeon or obstetrician attempting difficult and major medical procedures.

Colby (1951, p. 123) in a beginner's book on psychotherapy recommends that the couch be used in all possible circumstances, except perhaps if the patient is schizophrenic. He writes:

> To be under constant scrutiny means that some of your energy, which should be entirely devoted to the patient's communications, is shunted into efforts to guard your facial and bodily expressions. Using a couch does not automatically mean psychoanalysis nor does it necessarily demand free association.

A further illustration of the results of placing a schizophrenic on the couch is offered by another colleague J. Grigson (1976). The patient she refers to had spent many years in a mental hospital, then was seen as an out-patient at the facility where the colleague worked.

> A patient "over-dosed" on Melleril and was hospitalized. I visited her at the hospital to maintain the relationship with her. When she finally returned to my clinic she was very regressed, was silent, and slept a great deal. I began again to see her for one-half hour each week. At the first interview following hospitalization she walked into the office and said, "Where have you been all my life? That looks like a psychiatrist's couch!" I said, "Would you like to lie on it?" She did —in the fetal position. She was silent. I asked her what I should do when she was silent. She said, "Just sit there and be my guardian angel."
>
> So for three months this kind of interaction took place. She told me it was helpful to her for me to be silent and still. It had a calming and peaceful effect and she needed rest and relaxation. I would check half way through the interview asking, "How am I doing?"
>
> "Fine," she answered. Then one day when I asked what I should do, she said, "Just sit there and drink your coffee and smoke your cigarettes."
>
> Shortly after this she began talking. Now she talks for the entire interview and she is at a peak I have never seen her at before. The ripples of the treatment outside are: big improvement in church activities, and increased contact with friends. Last week she reported having sold items for the Brownies at a Bazaar and had a good time.

The analyst's skill includes not only the ability to assess the patient's condition but also his needs. This assessment together with the proper application of psychoanalytic technique should reward both the analyst and analysand with a considerable element of improved health both outside and inside the consulting room. In reporting on the final stage in the treatment of an originally very disturbed patient, Spotnitz (1967, p. 286) reports the following about the patient's behavior:

> The patient talks spontaneously, in an animated voice, and appears thoroughly at ease during the last six months of treatment. He lies on his back, arms and legs uncrossed; on occasion he may sit up on the couch by prearrangement, but he feels no need to behave impulsively during the session. He reports his current activities and tries to relate them to his memories of events in the remote past. Dreams are also reported regularly, and he participates actively in their analysis. The free associations of each session include reference to his sex life, and he talks freely of his thoughts and feelings about the analyst. He remains within the normal range of variability in attendance and payment of fees.

## THE TECHINQUE OF RESISTANCE MANAGEMENT

Once the question of whether a particular patient should be requested to use the couch is resolved in the analyst's mind, the next question is when to use it. My own inclination is to suggest that the patient lie on the couch in the first or second session unless some special situation seems to prevail. An example of such an exception would be a consultation with a relative or spouse who is in my office to discuss someone else. Another situation is with a person who is very cautiously exploring whether or not to begin treatment. Then I would suggest waiting for a number of sessions. In the latter case I often wait until the patients make some request for information about themselves of me and then I might answer, "Would you like to lie on the couch and discuss this?"

In any event, my introduction of the idea is usually in the form of a question. Typical of these might be, "Is it okay with you to lie on the couch?" "Would you object to using the couch?""What do you think about the idea of using the couch?"

Not all patients respond favorably to these questions. Many initially voice strong objections to doing so. Therefore, having made a decision to recommend to the patient that he or she use the couch, the analyst must then study the patient's reaction to the suggestion, then resolve and overcome the patient's resistance to following it. The key to the resolution of any resistance is to understand the origin, the history, and the meaning of it. This is easier said than done, but the fruits of the labor are not simply that the patient is lying on the couch, but that a major step forward in the treatment has been accomplished. The object, then, is not principally to get the patient on the couch, but to resolve the emotional conflicts that are represented in the resistances.

Many practioners and observers of the analytic process tend to misunderstand this objective in psychoanalysis. In principle, the analyst does not seek compliance. Rather he strives for ego development through the process of conflict resolution. Conflict resolution involves the releasing of emotional energy invested in objects and incidents no longer relevant to the "here and now" of life. The result is a reinvestment of these energies in processes that allow emotional growth to proceed. Compliance too often is the fore-runner of a passive–aggressive struggle for mastery at the anal level. This can reinforce the patient's conflicts and come home to roost in the form of a premature termination. Therefore, when the analyst offers the suggestion to the patient to use the couch he may invoke a conflict in the patient which can be represented in the form of a resistance to the request. A careful study by the analyst of this reaction to the suggestion cannot only reveal the story of the resistance, but its understanding can in itself be an important step forward in the analysis.

An example of the analyst and patient battling over the use of the couch was given to me by a student. He describes the case as follows:

A patient I had been treating for about seventy (70) sessions developed an extremely defiant attitude as a dominant aspect of his transference to me. He entered the office suddenly and sat on the far edge of the couch. Sitting there defensively huddled and with a determined jaw he announced that he was not going to lie on my sofa today and he did not want me to insist on it because it would do no good. I told him that he did not have to lie down, but I was curious why he chose to be so defiant today. He responded in a way that was heavily dramatized by head throwing and hand flinging, "Oh, all right! if you have to be this way, I'll lie on your sofa!" He half jumped up impulsively and threw his rear end toward the center of the couch, missed and went crashing to the floor with a thud. As he crawled back on the couch, he remarked, "God, I'm getting worse. You've got to help me."

Fortunately for me he continued talking and no response from me was necessary until I could be more objective.

Freud's (1927) five categories of resistence are useful guides for differentiating and understanding the basis for the resistance and ways to resolve it. These five catagories of resistances serve as excellent tools for the delineation and conceptualization of the patient's resistances to the use of the couch. The resistances are described followed by suggested solvents, analytic interventions, and examples:

| | |
|---|---|
| Id Resistances: | The repetition–compulsion principle is especially operative here and the patient fears some fantasy or wish being carried out or the repeating of actual, but perhaps forgotten, traumatic situations. The patient might say "I feel depressed lying here" or "I feel far away lying here" or "I would feel inferior lying there." |

Resistance Solvent:

This resistance is best resolved by bringing to consciousness what it is that is feared and then holding it out against the reality of the analytic situation.

Analytic Intervention:

Investigation—"What could go wrong being on the couch?" or "What threat does lying on the couch pose?"

Examples:

A young woman after starting treatment made it clear that she did not want to lie on the couch. She said, "I need to be able to see you when I speak with you." She would usually sit slouched in her chair in a sexually provocative posture. I asked her what especially did she want to see when she looked at me. She hesitated, then said my facial expression. I questioned whether my facial expression was interesting in terms of my initiating something in her or as a reaction to something she said or did. She said she was more concerned about my reaction to her. I asked what I might react to and she said she did not know and began talking about her job as a nurse. Later she complained about how uncomfortable she would become when men stared at her. I questioned why this was uncomfortable for her, and she said she felt that men would be undressing her with their eyes. I asked if I might be doing this. She laughed and said, "Of course not." I asked if she could lie on the couch and be secure I was not doing this. She replied affirmatively and went to the couch.

A medical student who entered treatment after a psychotic episode suffered from extreme shyness. He responded negatively to the question of whether he was interested in using the couch. When asked why he said he already felt very much alone and did not want to feel more alone. I questioned him as to whether he felt alone in actuality or in his mind. In other words, did he feel alone when he was in the classroom or only when he was in his apartment by himself. "Both places," he replied. I then explained that he really felt alone in his mind. When he agreed, I asked why he would be unwilling to lie on the couch since he would feel alone in his mind for the time being no matter what he did. He agreed and got on the couch.

Superego Resistance:     Through identification, usually unconscious, with a parent or other authority figure, judgments or stubborn attitudes are exhibited which interfere with the progress of the treatment. The patient might say, "If I were to lie on the couch it would be a sign of weakness," or "People should sit up and see each other when they talk," or "Why should you sit up and me lie down?"

Resistance Solvent:

This usually consists of an effort to explore with the patient the root of the idea. When the fixed idea is raised for logical examination, the patient usually yields to a reasonable request.

Analytic Intervention:

Exploratory—"Where did that idea come from?" or "What's wrong with me sitting up and you lying down? Why shouldn't it be that way?"

Examples:

A new patient entering my office said as she sat down in the chair opposite me, "You better not get the idea that I am going to lie down on that couch." I inquired, "Why shouldn't I get that idea?" "I just don't believe in psychoanalysis," she replied. "Then why did you want to see me?" I asked. "Well, my niece, Ethel, said you were very good and that you could help me because she had worse problems than me and you helped her." "Well, your niece Ethel used the couch and that seems to help her so why do you object to it?" I asked. She explained that she just did not want to be taken advantage of. I suggested that if I am the type of person who would take advantage of her perhaps she should seek someone else. She then acknowledged that since I did not take advantage of Ethel, I might not take advantage of her. I inquired as to how I could take advantage of her if I wanted to do so. She reluctantly told me, then laughed and expressed willingness to use the couch. Later, as the treatment progressed, her need to control, as part of her identification with her mother, revealed itself as playing a major part in her conflicts.

A graduate student in psychology declared it would be ridiculous for him to lie on the couch. He had read of a study where experts listening to tapes of sessions could not tell if the patients were sitting up or lying down. This showed the couch to be a useless piece of furniture. I asked why I keep useless pieces of furniture in my office, and his reply was that it's probably that the couch was useful, but that did not prove anything. I asked why I had such poor judgment. He said that perhaps I did not have the same opinion as the authors of the study. I asked why my opinion might be different and he thought it might be based on my experience. I asked him whether he would like to experiment and see what he could learn about the use of the couch. He said it could prove an interesting experiment and went to the couch. His conflict with authority figures played a prominent part in his analysis.

**Ego Resistance:** Synthesizing on a conscious level the information available, the patient reaches a positive or negative conclusion and then responds to a request with "yes I will" or "no I won't." The patient might say, "I would prefer not to use the couch."

**Resistance Solvent:** Providing the kind and amount of information that will persuade the patient to lie on the couch, usually resolves the hesitation.

**Analytic Intervention:** Explaining—"Did you know most people can relax better lying down?" and "Most people find the analysis goes better when they are on the couch."

Examples:

A professor in his initial interview stated "I would prefer not to use the couch." "How come?" I asked. "The couch is for sick people—neurotic people," he answered. "I only want to get some questions answered about myself." I asked him why he could not answer these questions himself. He explained that he had tried, but was unsuccessful and that is why he came to me. Perhaps, I could answer them. In questioning him further I was able to help him state that there were things about his behavior that could only be explained by making conscious certain feelings and ideas that at present seemed to elude him. I then asked him if he would want to try the couch if it might implement the process of making him more aware of his thoughts and feeling. He was then willing to use the couch.

A patient said he did not want to lie on my couch because he did not want to have to stare at the horrible painting I had on the wall facing the couch. I asked if he would be agreeable to using the couch if he did not have to see the painting. He answered yes. I then told him it would be all right to lie on the couch with his eyes closed. He laughed and went to the couch.

**Transference Resistance:**

This resistance is in some ways similar to an id resistance and utilizes the repetition-compulsion mechanism. Because the patient perceives the analyst as someone out of his past, he or she does not respond to the analyst or the analytic situation in a realistic way. Thus, the analyst has projected onto him motives and attitudes that are not accurate. "I feel you just want to use me," or "I wouldn't feel safe on a couch with you in the room" are typical examples of possible transference manifestations.

**Resistance Solvent:**

Helping the patient become aware of the distortion in the way the analyst is perceived and its roots in the past is usually helpful in dissolving this resistance.

**Analytic Intervention:**

Exploratory—"How do I plan to use you?" the analyst asks. "Why do I want to use you?" "Why am I that way?" "What kind of danger from me would you experience on the couch?" "Why would I want to hurt you?"

**Examples:**

After six months in treatment my patient declared that he would no longer lie on the couch and in fact was considering ending his treatment. I asked why, and he said he really couldn't stand me. I asked what was wrong, and he said it was my voice. My voice was intolerable to him. It was a terrible voice. In exploring this it turned out that my voice sounded like his voice. He had identified me with the negative parts of his personality and had formed a negative narcissistic transference to me which was very painful to him. I suggested that if perhaps he could stay with me and help me improve my personality, possibly there would be a chance for him to improve. He was very skeptical, but agreed to try.

A woman who had been in treatment about two years began experiencing much unexplainable anxiety whenever she lay down on the couch. It was difficult to comprehend its origin until she related a nightmare of a man coming into her bed at night and trying to choke her. Having her sit up when the anxiety became too intense helped her talk and work out her fear. Her talk led to a memory of her uncle having entered her bed when she was about fourteen years old. She was able to repulse his sexual advances, but he had threatened to choke her if she cried out. Prior to this incident she had felt attraction and admiration for her uncle. The development of similar feelings toward me led to the anxiety reaction on the couch.

**Secondary Gain Resistance:**

Because occasionally treatment can provide gains in larger measure than being out of it supplies, the patient can hesitate to accept a recommendation that can advance his progress or even take a step which appears like a commitment to treatment. Asked to use the couch he can say, "I'm not ready to do that yet," or "I just want to come in and talk to you. I don't want therapy."

**Resistance Solvent:**

It is beneficial to help the patient explore his real motives for coming to treatment and to explore future fears. The patient may out of guilt avoid becoming healthy and this should be investigated.

**Analytic Intervention:**

Exploring Future Fears—The analyst inquires, "What would happen if you were ready?" And, "Why can't you lie on the couch and talk to me?" "What would happen if you got therapy?" "Why aren't you good enough to use the couch?"

**Examples:**

The patient, a young graduate student, showed great reluctance to lying on the couch. At first he would give no reasons. He dismissed psychoanalysis as a farce. It subsequently came out that he was terrified of being inducted into the army and planned to use the treatment as a basis for being exempted from military service. His conflict was that while he did not want to be drafted, neither did he wish to acknowledge that he was a patient needing therapy. He wished to show his disdain for the government by eluding its attempts to induct him, and to show his disdain for psychoanalysis by engaging in a form of behavior that would escape its influence. He felt that to capitulate to the use of the couch would upset any gains the treatment could provide for him. I approached this problem from a number of directions. I told him it was unethical for me to treat someone who had no problems, I suggested that there probably were other doctors who would be pleased to have someone easy like him for a patient. I also suggested since he had no difficulties to discuss, at least the physical rest he obtained on the couch could be beneficial to his health. He then reluctantly decided to try using the couch. I helped him by encouraging him to talk about what he considered inconsequential matters. He became increasingly comfortable and talkative.

A man who had been in treatment for a number of years and who had made good progress asserted he no longer wished to use the couch. He no longer wished to delve deep in his mind and confront painful situations. I agreed with this and suggested we stop treatment. He did not want to do this because his wife might carry out her threat to leave him if he stopped. She had agreed to remain with him as long as he continued to try to improve his behavior. I then reassured him that he did not have to delve deep into his mind. He had done well in treatment and it only remained for him to demonstrate that he could have a pleasant comfortable relationship with me and that I would help him with this. When he expressed concern about his wife I reassured him on this issue too, telling him if he could have a good relationship with me, I was confident he could do so with his wife also.

It should be emphasized again that if the analyst is successful, he not only gets the patient to lie on the couch, but he simultaneously resolves the emotional conflict represented by this resistance to lying on the couch. When the analyst is committed to resistance analysis, he can find considerable satisfaction in successful efforts to discover, understand, and resolve those elements that are not the blocks to analytic progress they were once thought to be, but rather the building stones of a treatment of which he can be proud. Kubie (1950, p. 52) has said, "I would never feel entirely secure about an analysis in which the patient had never been able to use the couch." Also, patients who do utilize the couch in analysis invariably sit up for periods of time. Some of these situations have to do with extremely painful emotional reactions, undesirable regressions, colds, physical injuries, and requests to discuss certain matters.

In conclusion, the question of when or whether the couch should be used in a particular case must depend upon whether or not it conforms to the criterion of any psychoanalytic tool or technique and its usefulness in treatment; that is, its success in helping the analyst and analysand to bring the treatment to a positive therapeutic conclusion. The matter rests as much with the analyst's feelings toward the couch as with the mental condition of the patient. In no case is it certain that the use of the couch is especially prohibited. Its usefulness or harmfulness depends upon the training, skill, and attitudes of the therapist.

## Who Should Lie on the Couch?

In discussing pedagogical aspects of training analysis, Lewin (1973) believes that current methods of training analytic students tend toward reducing or eliminating

identification by the student with his analyst. He acknowl-
edges, however, that the student may identify with his analytic supervisor or even the institute. In his words (p. 501):

> An unresolved identification with the training analyst oc-
> curred more frequently in the "patriarchal" days, when an
> institute might be dominated by one or a few persons, and
> is of rarer occurrence among institute students now. Here
> the transference may be spread as if to an institution, but
> ordinarily comes to be resolved by the well-known process
> of working through. The model taken for emulation need
> not be the training analyst. Ekstein (1953) remarks that a
> supervisor often serves as an identication model.

Aside from unresolved identifications with the training
analyst, supervisor, or institute there are, nevertheless, a
number of unwritten codes of psychoanalytic procedure
and beliefs. These are aspects of procedure that are taught
by teacher to student in the "oral tradition." A significant
point about the oral tradition is that by being passed on by
word of mouth it can begin to lose the support and benefit
of being rooted in theory. The neglect or avoidance of
theory can lead to the stultification of the science. The
psychoanalytic student is more interested in learning technique, "how to do it," than he is theory. This stimulates
teaching in the "oral tradition." Many of these teachings
are seldom put into print. Here are some of them along
with commentaries.

a) If the patient is seen less than a given number of
times per week (recently the number is three), the couch
should not be used. The reason often given for this is that
less than, say, three analytic visits per week is not psychoanalysis, and since the process is not deemed to be psychoanalysis the couch should not be utilized.

Freud (1914a, p. 16.) was very emphatic about what
formed the basis of psychoanalytic treatment and stated:

It may thus be said that the theory of psychoanalysis is an attempt to account for two observed facts that strike one conspicuously and unexpectedly whenever an attempt is made to trace the symptoms of a neurotic back to their sources in his past life: the facts of transference and of resistance. Any line of investigation, no matter what its direction, which recognizes these two facts and takes them as the starting point of its work may call itself psycho-analysis, though it arrive at results other than my own.

If the process essential to psychoanalysis is the recognition and investigation of resistance and transference, then any means applied to this end could reasonably be called psychoanalysis regardless of the frequency of sessions.

Selesnick (1967, pp. 192–193) in reviewing some of the revisions of technique which were explored by the Chicago group of psychoanalysts says:

> Alexander, French, and their colleagues at the Chicago Psychoanalytic Institute advocated in their book *Psychoanalytic Therapy* (1946) that the rigid distinctions between psychoanalysis and psychotherapy be abandoned. Alexander remarked that "French was the first among us to state explicitly that there is no essential difference between the various procedures, that the difference lies merely in the extent to which the various therapeutic principles and techniques are utilized. We are working with the same theories (in psychotherapy and psychoanalysis)" [Alexander, 1964, p. 7]. He further explained that "what makes the procedure psychoanalytic is ... that it is based on psychoanalytic knowledge. What makes it psychoanalytic is that the therapist knows what is going on in the patient and knows what he is doing in terms of existing psychodynamic knowledge" [Alexander, 1962, pp. 176–177]. To consider treatment psychoanalytic merely because a patient reclines on a couch and is seen by an analyst a certain number of fifty-minute hours per week over many years means relying on format and superficial criteria. Alexander and French (1946) predicted that, in opposition to standardized procedure, a new flexible orientation was on its way, "according to which the various

forms of psychotherapy as well as the classical psychoanalytic procedure are considered as different applica-
tions of the universally valid principles of psychodynamics"
[Alexander, 1950, p. 4].

Since it appears that there have been no studies to
determine the minimum number of hours per week necessary to the analytic process, it could be asserted that in
terms of the transference, as in any relationship, frequency
of contact can determine the intensity of feelings produced
in both parties. Since intense feelings are very critical in the
transference, a good argument can be given in favor of
frequent meetings, but the optimum and the minimum
number are matters subject to discussion, and are not scientific certainty at this time.

b) A corollary of this could be that if the couch is being
used as part of the technique, the therapy could per se be
defined as psychoanalysis because only in psychoanalysis is
the couch employed as part of the technique along with the
study of transference and resistance. In other words, the
use of the couch in itself defines the type of treatment.

This perception of the type of treatment being defined
by whether or not the patient lies on a couch should be
abandoned. It should rather first be determined whether or
not the procedure being implemented in the process of
treatment is one where resistances and transference are
investigated and then consider whether the couch is a useful instrument in this process. Freud's own fairly successful
self-analysis carried out by mail with Wilhelm Fliess and the
self-study of his dreams should raise some doubts about the
issue of whether the couch is essential to this process. In
an experiment Hall and Closson (1964) found that experienced judges given tape-recorded sessions could not
differentiate sessions in which the patient was lying down
—even though the judges were quite confident of having
made this differentiation.

c) Because classical psychoanalysis requires and encourages the development of an object transference, a kind of transference most narcissistic individuals are not capable of, patients with preoedipal disorders such as alcoholics, addictions, schizophrenic, and borderline individuals are not considered suitable for psychoanalytic treatment. This being so, it is thought these people should not be put on the couch. It is further suggested that too much regression which could be damaging is fostered in such patients by using the couch.

Chessick (1971) did an intensive study of fourteen patients diagnosed as borderline (excluding adolescents and those who showed serious depressive tendencies, paranoia, or chaotic anxiety) and used the couch during psychotherapy sessions of two visits per week. He asserts that four patients became much worse and had to sit up after a few sessions. Two patients showed no detectable change. Six showed definite improvement. Two left therapy after a few months, although it was not known if this was in any way connected with the use of the couch.

Boyer (1966, p. 178) has written of his treatment of psychotic patients on the couch:

> When a person lies down on the couch, his visual contacts with the therapists' are diminished abruptly and he maintains contact primarily through hearing. Thus, the attitudes of the analyst, as reflected in his words, voice tones, and other sounds, assume great importance, and cannot be disguised. As with the pregenital child, particularly the child who has not yet learned to communicate with words, the introjections of the analysand are dependent upon the actual attitudes and qualities of the analyst. The psychotic patient wishes consciously to validate his auditory perceptions through their perceptual experience, notably visual and tactile, and sometimes presses to be allowed to sit, he develops anxiety which stimulates and emergence of data, serving the analytic purpose. Patients have verbalized subse-

quently their gratitude that they had not been encouraged
to face or touch me.

He (p. 179) writes further of the benefits of using the
couch with psychotics:

> Patients have commonly said that their remaining on the
> couch had made them aware of the magical nature of their
> fears of being destroyed by me or of destruction of me which
> at times they sought to achieve through fusion via tactile or
> visual contact.

Marmor (1962) has emphasized the importance of object relationships and of improving the communications
process as well as the need to resolve the transference. He
(p. 202) writes as follows:

> The fundamental problem involved, it seems to me, is how
> we can best facilitate the communication process, both ver-
> bal and non-verbal, between patient and therapist. If the use
> of the couch has any value at all, it is because it does indeed
> facilitate the process of communication for many patients.
> Thus, for dependent, compliant personalities who guide
> their every word by anxiously watching the expression on
> the analyst's face for approval or disapproval, the partial
> separation from the analyst offered by the couch is of great
> value. On the other hand, for the emotionally detached pa-
> tient who tends to avoid intimate human relationships, the
> couch may offer a refuge into which he can withdraw even
> further; and for such patients it may be of the utmost impor-
> tance therapeutically to work in a more direct face-to-face
> manner. The important thing is for the analyst to adapt his
> technique to the needs of the patient, rather than to be
> rigidly bound by a technical ritual regardless of its applica-
> bility. Indeed, I have a strong conviction that even if a pa-
> tient does communicate more freely lying on the couch, it is
> therapeutically important and valuable at some time or
> other in the analysis to have him also sit up and face thera-
> pists for a period of time. It is a truism in field theory that
> when you change the position of objects in a field you tend
> to change their relationships. Changing the position of the

patient often causes subtle but significant changes in his relationship to the therapist and in the pattern of his communications. It is not uncommon, for example, to find that transference anxieties which have been concealed by the safe detachement offered by the couch emerge quite clearly when the patient is asked to sit up and face the therapist. For these reasons, I have arrived at a conviction that, optimally, no analysis ought to be terminated without affording the patient an opportunity to resolve the transference in a normal face-to-face relationship with the analyst.

It is true that most psychotic, or narcissistic (pre-oedipal) patients are inherently, at least at the start of treatment, incapable of object transference, but increasing evidence indicates that such patients are capable, in time, of developing such a transference (Spotnitz, 1969, 1976). The treatment of the pre-oedipally fixated patient requires the analysis of resistance and narcissistic transference in order to facilitate the development of object transference. This treatment process, widely defined, could be designated psychoanalysis. If it can be demonstrated either that the use of the couch can be helpful or at least that it is not harmful, its use should not be ruled out. There are methods proposed by which the degree of regression can be regulated by the analyst treating both neurotic and psychotic patients, thereby reducing the likelihood of damaging the patient either while having the patient sit up or while using the couch (Spotnitz, 1969).

d) Similar considerations are applied to the treatment of children. It is thought that children cannot develop proper object transference and therefore the use of the couch is ruled out for them. Additional factors are that the use of the couch is dependent upon verbal communication, while with children play activity is deemed best. Also many children and adolescents are thought to be too restless to lie on the couch.

In contrast to this view there are some beliefs that

children can develop object transference (Bloch, 1974, Spotnitz 1976). Children like adults can suffer a variety of possible pathologies, therefore the use of the couch should not entirely be ruled out. Rather, because some children make excellent analytic progress lying on the couch, and enjoy its use, the employment of the couch should be kept in mind as a possibility for each child. There is nothing inherent in the basic psychoanalytic theory that rules out the use of the couch for children.

In conclusion, while the basis for the adherence to many of the particular procedures pertaining to the use of the couch has heretofore derived from the oral tradition, it is hoped that by the disciplined application of existing knowledge of psychoanalytic theory to the phenomena of the recumbent position, more clear, precise and concrete guidelines can be developed which ultimately will provide more positive therapeutic results.

# Chapter 10

# THE RELATION OF THE COUCH TO THE GOALS OF TREATMENT

## THE RELATION OF THE COUCH TO THE GOALS OF PSYCHOANALYSIS

As a mode of treatment psychoanalysis has certain concrete and precise objectives; as a method of research, it encompasses more abstract objectives.

Psychoanalysis for those who are practicing it professionally, has as its aim the treatment and cure of emotional disorders. As distinct from this, the aim of the science is to bring to light new evidence which can result in an improved theoretical understanding of the human psyche. Since the treatment and cure of patients take first priority for the clinican the scientific goals are necessarily secondary to them.

The use of the couch should be retained as long as it contributes to the specific cure of the patient. The understanding of the total curative process, as formulated within the science of psychoanalysis, includes a thorough knowledge of the functioning of its various elements. The continued use of the couch in treatment hinges upon scientific evidence that it provides definite benefits for both the patient and analyst.

Some contemporary analysts believe that the object of treatment is to develop the capacity for mature relationships. Such analysts believe that the capacity to sustain mature relationships naturally includes the ability to perceive oneself and others in terms of how one really is and how other people really are free from neurotic distortion.

Fairbairn (1958) argues that from the start of the treatment the attainment of mature relationships is one of the important goals of the patient, and since the recumbent position is detrimental to this effort, he therefore treats his patients in an upright position. Because under ordinary circumstances mature people do not relate to each other on the basis of one or more individual reclining, it is therefore reasoned that the use of the couch is antithetical to the achievement of maturity. Consequently, the use of the couch is discouraged by him and other therapists who agree with him.

When it is asserted that having a patient lie down on a couch makes a child out of him, the implication is that this posture is not that of an adult, but that of a child. A corollary of this is that sitting up represents the posture of an adult while lying down is infantilizing. To the extent that lying down infantilizes people and having them sit matures them, this information, if true, could be very useful.

There does not seem to be any evidence that lying down or sitting up, aside for the purpose of sleep, plays a significant part in the physical or emotional growth of a child. If this is true, the recumbent position is irrelevant to the question of maturity. It could be argued that although attaining mature relationships may be one of the aims of treatment, particularly for some patients, the posture of the participant is not necessarily relevant to this goal. Having a child sit up is not likely to be an important factor in a child's emotional growth nor in itself make a person an adult and, conversely, having an adult recline does not in itself make a child of him. Conceivably a person might feel like an adult when sitting up and feel like a child when lying down; however, feelings do not determine one's maturity. If one considers that access to all feelings along with constructive behavior is one aspect of maturity, then a form of therapy which allows the full expression of feelings and limits activity to constructive communication is most likely to be successful. Although the couch limits physical movement, it places no restraint on full verbal communication.

Another point of view is that the analyst's personality in itself has a powerful curative effect. Following this view the maximum exposure of the therapist to the patient would be beneficial and the couch in this situation would be contraindicated.

Robertiello (1967, p. 70) who emphasizes the importance of the analyst's personality makes a low assessment of those who insist on using the couch and characterizes them as follows:

> The therapist says "Yes, I like it that way too, I'm uncomfortable with a real involvement with a person too. This way I can make money, have status and express intellectual interpreations about you without having to ever get my feet wet or my hands soiled by touching you physically or emotionally. I'll be able to reinforce my own intellectual defenses against contact with people and feel I'm being an objective scientist and that this is the right and only way. Besides, if I ever let myself see you or you see me, it might get very sticky. You might find out that I'm as sick as you are and might leave me. And I might start to care about you or want you or hate you or need you and that would be very upsetting to both of us. Yes, by all means, let's continue to stay out of reach, never look at one another and play analyst."

Gruen (1967) responding to Robertiello's polemic in a moderate tone identifies his error in confusing the couch with the man. He suggests that a healthy therapist who is capable of interacting with his patients can do so regardless of whether a couch or a chair is used, and an unhealthy therapist cannot do so regardless of the circumstances. He points out that the man who uses the couch or a chair should be the center of focus, and the use of the couch must depend on whether the patient and therapist find it helpful in any given case.

There are many others who, in stressing the importance of the therapeutic personality in the treatment process, raise objections to the use of the couch. The nature of some of these objections and how the analyst responds to them deserve a critical and extended examination. These objections come not only from the general public, but also from other professionals. A further example of these objections and my responses to them is presented in the interest of illustrating and clarifying this matter (Stern and WIlson, 1974). Bradford Wilson, the author of the statements below, is a well-respected psychotherapist:

> Under the guise of preserving the therapist's anonymity as a "blank screen" onto which the client is free to project and project and project until he/she has distilled a distorted and many times-reinforced syndrome of monstrous magnitude known as the Transference Neurosis, the therapist is more often than not simply copping out on his own therapeutic responsibility for being a visably authentic human being in the presence of his clients. The therapist's insecurities about his or her own acceptability as a member of the human condition thus gets avoided and conveniently identified as "transference" on the part of the client, the reasoning being that "after all, if I've said nothing and done nothing and my face is not visible, then the client's so-called perceptions must not be perceptions at all, but must instead be projections!" The naive assumption here indulged in is the notion that "doing nothing" is a state of in-activity.
>
> I think much more is lost by eliminating the face-to-face interaction between the therapist and client than is gained by the presumed facilitation of the free-associative process by dint of the couch and the so-called Incognito.

I would like to take issue with the prevalent notion that a) the couch is somehow indispensible to free association, and b) that constant free-association is indispensible to good psychotherapy. With regard to (a), during the years when I used the couch with clients, I noted (on occasions when the client had physical conditions that precluded lying down— or else they just felt like sitting up for a change) that the quantity and quality of their associations remained the same and comparable. As for (b) most clients can only sustain free-association for about 10 or 15 minutes at a clip then they "come up for air" and analyze, evaluate, discuss, or interpret. It is during this evaluative (or feedback) phase of the session that the face-to-face interaction does most to help bridge the gap between fantasy and reality. Human beings rely very heavily on visual data (bodily gestures, facial expressions) for much of our communication. Drastically reducing communication between therapist and client is, to my way of thinking, counter-therapeutic. As noted before, it pushes the client deeper and deeper into autistic imaginings without benefit of authentic feedback.

The couch precludes the kind of therapist–client interaction which I consider to be the "workshop" part of the therapeutic session; both client and therapist gain much growth by dint of their collaborative efforts toward working through and living with their mutual interactions. Not to do so is to add to the unreal and other-worldly atmosphere which the couch situation is adept at promoting; as though there is one world out there and another kind of world in the therapist's office. Granted that the therapy session has many unique features which set it apart from the working day world, it is nevertheless a kind of exercise room, a milieu in which the client can flex muscles and undergo rehearsals for later behaviors out there, and rehearsing via the therapist–client interaction is an indispensable component of the healing process.

My third and final point has to do with passivity. Most clients come to us only after some of their pet defenses have failed. They come to us humiliated by that knowledge and with their early infantile grandiosity thoroughly activated and being turned upon us in full force—as though to say "I couldn't make my aberrant techniques work." Thus they come to us for "help," putting their worst (i.e., weakest, most helpless, most passive) foot forward. Some are even quite symbolic about it, peppering the intake process with requests for electroconvulsive therapy, hypnotherapy, injections, pills, and the like. My own very first dream after my first psychoanalytic session consisted of my lying strapped to an operating table in a vast darkened hall wherein could be heard the reverberations of a J. Arthur Rank gong followed by an echoing and sepulchral male voice intoning the words "You are now in psychoanalysis!"

Put another way, I believe that the couch posture smacks far too much of the medical (patient/doctor/treatment) model of psychotherapy which modern humanism is trying to outgrow. Lying on the couch says "do something for/to me" and the therapist, by encouraging such a posture, is giving tacit assent to such a notion while at the same time saying to the prone client "I'm interested in seeing you stand up and assert yourself." Small wonder that the couch method proved early on to be disastrous in the case of schizophrenics, schizoids, and character disorders—leading to Freud's gloomy conclusion that psychoanalysis is powerless to help these individuals. The mixed message just referred to is a rerun of the very same double bind situation which these people grew up in and which caused them a major part of their hassles in the first place. (During the past twenty years or so these clients have been accepted into classical Freudian modes of psychotherapy, but it has been axiomatic that such persons are "sit-up patients.").

## Excerpts of my response to Wilson's thoughts are presented here:

What I have found to be interesting in my study of the use of the couch is the way it has become a symbol and sometimes a scapegoat for what is actually a philosophy of how therapy should or should not be carried out. It is evident in your discussion—and I find this entirely agreeable—that you judge in large measure the usefulness of the couch based upon your own experiences in psychoanalytic treatment and upon your personal views of a valid therapeutic experience. So while we are presumably discussing the couch we may be actually concerned with the complicated fabric of psychoanalysis itself. In such a discussion we naturally grasp the tools that best shape our desired conclusions. A difficulty of this type of process is that the tools may not be interchangeable. Psychoanalysis employs a variety of tools that do not necessarily fit other therapies. This should not speak well of psychoanalysis nor badly of other therapies or vice versa. It is merely that the mechanics, the tools, the methods, and the objectives may be different. For example, how can a drug-oriented psychotherapist have much respect or tolerance for transference? The very idea would be antagonistic to his purpose of very brief encounters with his patients. But for the psychoanalyst, the transference phenomena is a basic and fundamental aspect of his practice. It is well known that if one wishes to encourage transference one withholds information about himself, and if he desires to dissolve transference he provides full information about himself. If he does the former he gets distortion and regression in the analytic hour which can be even further augmented by the use of the couch. The recumbent position being a closer approximation of the distortion and regression of sleep helps foster the transference phenomena. So far I hope I am not saying that this whole procedure is good or bad, but is a limited view of the total picture of how the treatment process works.

When you state that the therapist has the responsibility for being a visibly authentic human being in the presence of his clients, you are presenting a valid view of how treatment is to be carried out. In being authentic the therapist is not encouraging transference, but he is using a different tool to produce emotional improvement. For you the therapeutic incognito is antagonistic to your therapeutic objectives. Oil and water are not bad. They just do not mix.

The other issue, that of free association, is one where I generally agree with you. I do not believe the couch is indispensible for free association. Freud was able to free associate in his writing and was able to encourage this in patients and friends while taking walks. I'll go further and not only agree with you that free association is not indispensible to good psychotherapy, but is contraindicated when one wishes to maintain full orientation to reality. Free association can induce regression and is not desirable unless this is an objective of the treatment.

You are correct in pointing out that visual data are important aspects of the total range of communication that transpires between humans. I can appreciate that visual clues are indispensible tools in doing "authentic therapy."

In psychoanalysis we do not ignore visual communication: it is just that we place much more emphasis upon verbal and cognitive communication. We have in psychoanalysis concepts concerning intrapsychic structure. These concepts postulate intrapsychic communication id, ego, superego, which rests mainly upon verbal communication. To heighten this we are interested in inhibiting visual clues to the patient. The result of inhibiting external clues usually is the enlargement of internal perception.

What is being suggested here is that the use of the couch promotes a relationship that is certainly not typical of what usually transpires between two people. However, though the experience is not typical of a two-person (dyadic) relationship, this does not axiomatically make it "inauthentic." In fact, the opposite might be true. To the extent that the analysand says what he really thinks and what he really feels and at a deeper level than that he usually is in touch with, he may during this therapeutic experience be a more genuine individual than he is in most other circumstances. Progressively, as the treatment proceeds, he may come to be a genuine human being in all areas of his life.

The analyst too cannot be effective in his work unless he is genuinely in touch with the feelings and thoughts induced in him by the patient. Optimally, his own analysis will have freed him to be genuinely in touch with the accepting of his own personality.

Not only is it essential that these people try to be as genuine as possible in their feelings and thoughts, but also that the situation be focused on those feelings and thoughts of the moment, the "here and now." In this sense the transference (a phenomenon which represents a distortion of the real situation) is a resistance to the here and now and has to be analyzed and resolved. As you pointed out, the therapist does not "let it all hang out." In that it is his responsibility to manage the progress of the treatment, the analyst, though he will authentically be in touch with his feelings and thoughts, will optimally reveal only those which will promote the course of the treatment. This is very difficult to accomplish. Most therapists tend either to say too much or too little and not necessarily what is therapeutic for the patient.

This brings me to the idea of passivity. It is true that passivity prevails in the analytic relationship. But then, pas-

sivity prevails in some aspect of all relationships. Though
the person on the couch may be physically passive, he is
encouraged to be very active verbally. The greater burden
of passivity is upon the analyst who, though sitting up, is
enjoined against any activity except that which is therapeutic
for the patient, and then he may respond only with words.
On the couch the analytic patient is no more physically passive than if he were sitting up. It is only his position that is
different. I contend that it is not the use of the couch that
proves disastrous in the treatment of schizophrenics, schizoids, and character disorders, but rather the therapist's
failure to properly manage the regression. The modern pys-
choanalyst, through utilization of a number of therapeutic
interventions, can regulate the extent of his patient's regression whether or not the couch is used.

If the personality of the analyst in itself has an important curative effect outside of his experience, knowledge,
and therapeutic ability, this effect might be explained by a
symbolic meaning, such as God, that the analyst may have
for the patient. Too often analysts find themselves denying
to others that they play God with their patients. It is sufficient to bring reality to those people who see psychoanalysts as God, without giving further encouragement
to this point of view. To facilitate the God-complex by
holding forth the therapist's personality as any kind of
model in the interpersonal therapeutic relationship tends
more to deny the reality principle than to support it. If the
symbolic meaning of the analyst is not the element that is
curative, it is, or should be, the analyst as a real person who
has this effect. If it is the latter, it can be asked how the
analyst differs from any other real person in the patient's
life who might equally provide this benefit.

When the procedure is such that the personality of the
therapist is paramount to the therapy, then the treatment
cannot be considered to be psychoanalysis. In psychoanalysis what is foremost is the continued study of the communication process in terms of the transference and resistances.

It is sometimes maintained that because the use of the couch in psychoanalysis came into existence as a replacement for hypnosis at a very different time, place, and social climate, it is a social and therapeutic anomaly today. It is further asserted that changes in therapeutic orientation and technique make the use of the supine position outmoded. Braatøy (1954, p. 117) comments about this change in orientation:

> In the analysis of psychoanalysis the most provoking phenomenon is that Freud, the archrationalist in the field of irrational behavior, took over from hypnosis, from what he himself regarded as an irrational psychotherapy, the supine position of the patient on the couch. He did this without questioning why this part of the set-up might be important to the patient. He simply stated that this part is "what is left over from hypnotic treatment." [Freud, 1913b, p. 97] The rational arguments he gives in the same connection have only to do with the importance of this ceremonial to the analyst. With this background it becomes understandable that Franz Alexander and his group in Chicago could publish a book on psychoanalytic therapy in 1946 where they suddenly, and again without specifying rational reasons, leave out the couch as a means of treatment. It is nevertheless a curious fact, remembering that the Chicago group more than any other psychoanalytic branch has stressed the somatic aspects, because the couch is continually and directly influencing the muscles (literally, the soma) of the patient. The couch, that is, the supine position, influences from the first moment and as long as it is used the tonus of the muscles and "morphogenetically, as well as physiologically (muscle tonus) is a master function."

Many good reasons for avoiding the use of the couch with the psychotherapist behind are given by Fromm-Reichmann (1950). She not only believes that this relationship opens the door too widely to the possibility of the therapist napping during the patient's session, but she also feels that advances in psychoanalytic insight and technique permit more active intervention than the earlier colorless and inanimate appearances some analysts endeavor to portray. She believes that the therapist can accomplish more by facing the patient. Basically, Fromm-Reichmann maintains that changes in analytic orientation as to theory and methods of treatment require concomitant changes in the physical relationship between patient and therapist. She concludes that although the use of the couch makes the analyst feel more comfortable it does not mean this arrangement is better for the patient.

A frequent criticism of psychoanalysis is that it plays too much in the dust of the past and seeks solutions in history, rather than directing attention to where the problems lie, in the present. The problems of most people lie in either or both of two areas, the way they feel and the way they behave. In psychoanalysis there is an attempt to understand the origin and meaning of the patient's feelings and behavior. People do have problems in the here and now. Analytic therapy does not avoid the here and now, but on the contrary attempts to place the floodlights of attention upon it. Whereas the face-to-face position tends to direct the relationship to a "here and now" time focus, the analytic goals are to bring into expression the distortions and projections characterologically used by the patient in the "here and now." It is this fluidity and kaleidoscopic change in the patient's thoughts from present to past, present to future, as he reaches inward and outward, that we wish to encourage both in and out of treatment.

Trends in psychotherapy are such that the previous sharp distinction between what has been known as psychoanalysis and what has been called psychoanalytic psychotherapy fades as times goes on.

Forty years ago one either was a psychoanalyst or one was not. If you were a psychoanalyst your patients used the couch; if all your patients did not use the couch you were not an analyst. Today it is different. Analysts for the most part have expanded the range of disorders they wish to work with and feel confident in treating. Also, the physical setting is different. Many analysts work in clinics, hospitals, and community centers where it is not possible to use the recumbent position. There is in these settings increasing emphasis on working with larger numbers of people and in group therapy. These demands do not invalidate psychoanalytic therapy. They call for more training and versatility on the part of the therapists. This trend which has been studied by many, (Nelson, 1965) is likely to continue.

In discussing the recent developments in psychoanalysis, Kanzer and Blum (1976, p. 103) say:

> The classical psychoanalytic setting and procedure have undergone little change among analysts who seek a fundamental revision of the personality through: (1) the establishment of conditions that favor the development of a transference neurosis; (2) the resolution of the neurosis through interpretation and working through. Nevertheless, "the most profitable view to adopt toward the analytic technique seems to consider the use of the couch, free association, the handling of the transference, the handling of the transitional forms of acting out, etc., as mere tools of treatment"; and, as Anna Freud (1954) has pointed out, "tools of any trade are periodically inspected, reviewed, sharpened, perfected, and, if necessary, altered. As in all other cases, alterations would not be carried out arbitrarily and without sufficient cause."

Another element nonexistent in its present form 40 years ago and earlier is the appeal of research. Not the sort of research Freud engaged in by studying his own dream life or that of Ferenczi, the brilliant innovator, who experimented in his office laboratory, but the kind of research amenable to statistical analysis and carried out by large numbers of researchers. Where the emphasis on research is on the ascendency, interest in psychoanalysis tends to decline. Research demands facts, figures, proof, and familiarity with statistics. Psychoanalysis which is limited to verbal interchange of an often symbolic nature is not amenable to the usual measurement approaches to research. Most psychoanalytic research in the past has been of the descriptive or case study method. This method cannot benefit from the application of large numbers of people, observers, or sums of money. It therefore does not attract eager young researchers. They are likely to become involved in areas of study that could absorb more people and money such as behavioral psychology.

Today, research is performed jointly by two or more people, supported in large part by government funds and taking place in laboratories, university classrooms, or hospital facilities using one-way mirrors, tape recorders, and computers. The concept of doing research has increasing allure to young therapists. It has not only prestige, but the assurance of steady income, at least for the period of the research project.

Henry A. Murray, Professor Emeritus at Harvard, one of the founders of the Boston Psychoanalytic Society, has observed (Hall, 1968, p. 58) the change: "Generally speaking, only a very few American academic psychologists have got around to being interested in human nature as it operates internally and covertly. The major aim of most of the bright young graduate students in psychology seems to be to demonstrate that they are strictly objective scientists."

Robertiello (1967) considers it a funny thing that the use of the couch arises out of what he considers to be an accident, Freud's transition from using the couch for hypnosis to using it for psychoanalysis. As others have pointed out, serendipity has been no liability for science, and truth has at least as often been liberated by accident as it has by alleged intended logical direction (Bratwaite, 1960; Bronowski, 1965).

Unfortunately, psychoanalysis is not very amenable to being researched, at least by outside observers. to date the large numbers of variables that encompass analytic parameters have not been sufficiently tamed to come up with uniform hypotheses that are valid and reliable. For this psychoanalysis may be penalized by losing possible adherents. And the couch will likely be seen as an important emotional vehicle, not having statistically demonstrated its worth.

## PATTERNS OF CHANGE

There are a number of other schools of psychotherapy, that not only actively promote their own methods of therapy, but also vigorously denounce psychoanalysis with all its accoutrements such as the couch, resistances, and transference. These attackers often do not confine their criticisms to footnotes, but treat psychoanalysis as an enemy to be assaulted in the first paragraph. The validity of their allegations is as important as the degree to which an unknowledgeable public is influenced by them. The damage would appear to be more significant in terms of those who consider becoming therapists, than those who consider becoming patients. There will be no lack of the latter.

At first Freud saw each patient for six full hours each week, and then when he reached age 65 reduced the frequency to five times per week. The custom of patients seeing their analyst five times a week seems to be diminishing. Glover (1955) has pointed out that analysts have a tendency to fit analysis more to the reality of their own needs than to those of their patients and call it by the same term. But the truth is that many more analysts seem to be seeing more patients fewer times per week and refer to this therapy as psychoanalysis. There need be no argument with this, but 40 years ago less than three or four sessions a week was not psychoanalysis and one did not use a couch. A number of very good therapists who use the couch and insist their therapy is psychoanalysis are known to see patients once per week and once every two weeks for 50 minutes. Among analysts the rules vary considerably governing the question of which patients are to lie on the couch, when they are to begin this, and under what circumstances they should be asked to sit up. The criteria for applying these rules is sometimes very complicated and depends on the philosophy and orientation of the analyst.

Hollander (1965, p. 56) has commented further on who might use the couch:

> In the mind of the general public it is as much the symbol of psychoanalysis as the striped pole is of barbering. It has become a guild symbol for some psychoanalysts who would maintain that only persons with the proper credentials are entitled to use it. Actually, too much meaning has been placed on the couch in practice as well as in *New Yorker* cartoons. There is no reason why the couch cannot be used on occasion by non-analysts.

Roazen (1975, p. 388) discusses Freud's fear for the future of psychoanalysis and measures the actual historical turn of events by the way the couch is used. He says:

> Freud's forebodings about what would happen to his ideas in America have been in some measure fulfilled. For example, in the consulting rooms of present-day British analysts, the analytic couch is prominently displayed, sometimes in the very center of the room. When one moves across the Atlantic to New England, the analytic couch, still a distinct entity, is more likely to be inconspicuous, placed against a wall. In Chicago an analyst's couch might be used for social purposes as well as therapeutic ones, and on the West Coast the furniture of the analyst's office—which is likely to include enough chairs for group therapy—makes abundantly clear just what Freud feared, that to the analyst the practice of analysis has become one therapeutic technique among many others.

The couch is the only instrument that the analyst uses, other than his mind and voice. Any therapeutic device used with skill and understanding is presumed to be of greater meaning to the therapist and has the possibility of providing him with more confidence as he goes about his work. The final decision as to the appropriateness of the use of the couch will rest with the therapist, rather than categorical imperatives about its use. Either the use of the couch is of little importance one way or another, an empty trademark, or else it is a tool of sufficient utility that should not be used without full understanding of precisely those potential effects it can produce in each patient.

Finally, the future trends of psychoanalysis depend upon developments in theory. We are a restless profession who continually reexamine our texts and our methods. New developments have occurred and no doubt will again. New theories will be created, tested, and ultimately influence our direction. To date, the couch has survived changes in theory, technique, and therapeutic intensity. As with the other visissitudes in the profession, the use of the couch will hopefully be dependent upon its continued contribution to the therapeutic goal of treating the most people most successfully in the shortest period of time. The use of the couch will either continue to flow with this stream, or it will be washed on the shore by progress.

Statistical estimated analysis of practicing professionals engaged in psychotherapeutic disciplines:

a)  about 35,000 members of the American Psychiatric Association
b)  about 10,000 members of the American Psychological Association doing clinical work
c)  about 5,000 members of the National Association of Social Workers who practice psychotherapy
d)  about 2,000 members of the American Psychoanalytic Association
e)  about 500 members of the National Association for Accreditation in Psychoanalysis

# REVIEW OF THE LITERATURE

## The History of the Use of the Couch: Developments in Psychoanalytic Theory and Practice

Useful as background reading to the history of the use of the recumbent position by ancient healers and modern hypnotists have been writings by Halpern (1963) describing Socrates humorous use of the couch, Zilboorg and Henry (1941), who provide a thorough history of medical psychology; Kline (1958), who explores specifically the issue of Freud and hypnosis; Alexander and Selesnick (1966), who explore in depth the history of psychiatry; Goshen (1967), who provides a comprehensive survey of psychiatry in a documentary style; Ellenberger (1970) who explores in great detail the giants in this field and their contributions, and Thompson (1950) who traces the evolution and development of psychoanalysis.

## FREUD'S WRITINGS ON HYPNOSIS

Freud's own comments on the use of hypnotic therapy and its eventual abandonment in favor of psychoanalysis are expressed in the following of his writings: (1888), a preface to the translation of Bernheim's suggestive techniques; (1889), a review of August Forel's text on hypnotism; (1891), a discussion of hypnosis as a technique for cure; (1892a), the presentation of a case of successful treatment by hypnotism; (1892b) the preface and footnotes to the translation of Charcot's Tuesday lectures; (1895), a text with Josef Breuer on a new method of treatment of hysteria by lifting repression; (1901), in an autobiographical note he regards himself as a pupil of Brucke and Charcot; (1904), he discusses the replacement of hypnosis with psychoanalysis and says that he does not despise hypnosis and suggestion, but he is loyal to psychoanalysis which he himself founded; (1905a), he contrasts hypnosis which is not concerned with resistance resolution with psychoanalysis which is; (1914), reasons for giving up hypnosis are described; and (1925), he describes having abandoned hypnosis, but he retains the use of the couch.

## FREUD'S WRITINGS ON THE COUCH

The writings in which Freud makes reference to the use of the couch seem to be limited to the following: (1912), wherein he writes of the advantage of the analyst maintaining a posture of free-floating attention enabling him to thereby best use his own unconscious processes, and (1913), where he refers to the couch as a ceremonial observance and as a leftover from hypnosis, explains his distaste for being gazed at, and describes the advantage of the couch in understanding and resolving certain resistances.

## WRITINGS ABOUT FREUD'S USE OF THE COUCH

Jones (1953) has provided a wealth of background on Freud himself, his times, and the setting in which the couch came to be used for psychoanalysis. Braatøy (1954) has made an attempt to understand the use of the couch in terms of its beginnings with Freud and its subsequent basis in technique. Millett (1962) explores the use of the couch in terms of other analysts' emulation of Freud. Alexander and Selesnick (1966) provide extensive historical background in the entire field of psychiatry and include Freud's own development. Coltrera and Ross (1967) and Gedo and Pollock (1967) also explore the basis for Freud's use of the couch. The Wolf-Man (1971) as a long term patient of Freud's is able to supply a number of personal observations and quotes from Freud regarding the use of the couch. Shur (1972), who for a long time was personal physician to Freud, also provides much firsthand knowledge of Freud and his views. Finally, Roazen (1975) has investigated in considerable detail Freud's reasons for using the couch. He furnishes a rationale other than the well known direct quotes from Freud.

## ARTICLES DIRECTLY ABOUT THE COUCH

Kelman (1954) describes the physical positioning of the couch in terms of the office setting and explores whether the couch is better than the chair. Hall and Closson (1964) report that experienced judges when listening to tape-recorded sessions could not differentiate sessions in which the patient was sitting up from those in which the patient was lying down, even though the judges were quite confident they had succeeded in doing so. Robertiello (1967) is emphatically against the use of the couch which he sees as a means by which the therapist defends himself from really getting emotionally involved with patients. Gruen (1967) in response to Robertiello cautions against confusing the couch with the man. Thus, he maintains, a healthy therapist should be capable of interacting with his patients regardless of whether a couch or a chair is used during the therapy session. Rosenbaum, S., (1967) discusses the significance of the couch very convincingly and thoroughly. He informs us of the symbolic meaning and provides thoughts concerning the benefits and limitations as to its use. Chessick (1971) reviews some of the arguments in the literature concerning the use of the couch and describes his experiences in private practice utilizing the recumbent position with 14 patients diagnosed as borderline. He concludes it is not the use of the couch that is important, but the abilities and inclinations of the psychotherapists.

## PSYCHOANALYTIC THEORY

Authors who have written about aspects of psychoanalytic theory that have relevance to the use of the couch are as follows:

Freud (1915), writing about the unconscious processes of the mind, describes his concept of topography. This concept explains the fluidity of attention to various levels of consciousness. In a later paper, he (Freud, 1917) discusses his theory of repression and its significance in neurosis. Anna Freud (1946a) develops the theory of defensive mechanisms which protect the ego from various kinds and sources of anxiety. Reich (1949) discusses the influence of the recumbent position on body muscular tension. Kris (1951) speaks of the phenomena of regression in the service of the ego. Jones (1953) explains in broad terms the development of Freud's theories. Braatøy (1954) explores in great depth the principle of relaxation and the physical implications of the use of the couch. Shur (1958), too, is concerned with the occurrence of regression. Waelder (1964) discusses the relationship of theory to technique. Zubek and MacNeill (1967) investigate the phenomenon of perceptual isolation which is induced by the use of the recumbent position, Lewin (1973) describes the meaning of sleep related to the couch, and Spotnitz (1969) discusses how the use of the couch can facilitate communication.

## TECHNIQUE AND THE USE OF THE COUCH

Some psychoanalytic writers have made useful comments about the use of the couch or some aspect of technique. Freud (1912) recommends for the analyst that he remain suspended in a position of "free-floating attention." He explains (1913) his aversion to being gazed at and recommends the use of the couch. A number of writers discuss different ways of introducing the patient to the couch. Among these are Braatøy (1954), Greenson (1967), Guntrip (1971), Spotnitz (1969).

On the subject of sleep, Fromm-Reichman (1959) is strongly against the use of the couch because she feels it encourages the analyst to sleep. Ferenczi (1926), quoting Freud to support his view, asserts the danger resulting from the analyst sleeping is not very great. Perls (1969) sees nothing wrong with a therapist sleeping.

A number of writers focus on the physical setting of the analyst's office and the positioning of the chair and couch. Among these have been Braatøy (1954), who emphasizes the importance of having the patient in full view; Greenacre (1971), who discusses the physical arrangement of the office and the use of the couch; and Kelman (1954), who recommends flexibility in the positioning of the analyst and the patient.

In considering whether certain kinds of patients should be ruled out as far as being placed on the couch, many analysts have strong and varying opinions. Anna Freud (1946b) and Melanie Klein (1954) do not recommend the use of the couch for children. Boyer (1966) found he was able to treat many psychotics successfully on the couch. On the other hand, Saul (1958) opposes the use of the couch for schizoid personalities. Chessick (1971) recommends the use of the couch for selected borderline patients. Caligor and Wittenberg (1967) do not recommend putting obsessive-compulsive patients on the couch. Spotnitz (1969) believes the personality of the therapist, not the patient, is the important variable in whether patients should be treated on the couch. He recommends the use of the couch with schizophrenic patients.

## CULTURAL INFLUENCES ON THE USE OF THE COUCH

Some writers have been helpful in examining the role of the couch in the cultural stream in which psychoanalysis finds itself. Kurt Adler (1967) discusses the idea that the chair and the couch introduces the idea of superior and inferior. Bion (1958) discusses the significance of looking for the psychotic patient. Bateson and Ruesch (1951) explore the asymmetries of the analytic situation where the analyst can look and the patient cannot. Sharpe (1950) and Szasz (1957) claim it is beneficial for the analyst to get pleasure in looking, listening, exploring, and imagining. Greenson (1967) explains how the analyst's excessive discomfort at being looked at can cause the analyst too early and inappropriately to place the patient on the couch.

Gerhard Adler (1967) sees the couch as a symbol of psychoanalysis, as does Spotnitz (1961). Circot (1962) describes the science of symbolism.

Freud (1905b) introduces and pioneers in the recognition of the psychology of humor. Grotjahn (1957) shows how wit can be a disguised expression of aggression.

Borosen and Ginsberg (1967) review and categorize various types of psychiatric jokes. Redlich and Bingham (1953) examine jokes in larger social settings as an expression of the public's fear and anger at psychiatry.

## THE RELATIONSHIP OF THE COUCH TO THE GOALS OF TREATMENT

In considering the goals of psychoanalysis and the future use of the couch in psychoanalysis, the following authors have been of help:

Blum and Kanzer (1967) believe the classic psychoanalytic setting will not likely change extensively among psychoanalysts who operate through interpretation, working through resistances, and the development and the resolution of the transference neurosis. Anna Freud (1954) considers the couch among the "tools of the trade" of psychoanalysis. She is of the opinion that although these tools should be periodically inspected, changes should not occur arbitrarily and without sufficient cause. Roazen (1975) believes that Freud's concern that his ideas would suffer corruption in America have in some ways been confirmed. Braaty (1954), discussing the divergent development of the Chicago group under Alexander and Freud, believes that this is an example of the weakening in America of Freud's ideas.

Revealing a tendency in America to shift the goals of treatment, Robertiello (1967) states that it is the personality of the therapist that is the main agent for change in treatment and therefore the analyst should remain in full view of the patient. Gruen (1967) responding to this view says that when the personality of the therapist is paramount, the treatment ceases to be psychoanalysis. Marmor (1962) believes that communication between the analyst and the patient is a paramount goal in the treatment. Since this is so, he suggests that each analysis should include a period when patient and analyst are face to face.

Hollander (1965), assessing the positive aspects of the use of the couch, suggests that it could beneficially be used by nonpsychoanalysts.

Hall (1968), in reporting the views of the distinguished American psychologist Henry Murray, relates that contemporary therapists are more interested in being objective scientists than they are in dealing with human nature.

# REFERENCES

Adler, G. Methods of treatment in analytical psychology. In B. Wolman (Ed.), *Psychoanalytic techniques.* New York: Basic Books, 1967.

Adler, K. Adler's individual psychology. In B. Wolman (Ed.), *Psychoanalytic techniques.* New York: Basic Books, 1967.

Ahsen, A. Personal communication, 1966.

Alexander, F. Analysis of the therapeutic factors in psychoanalytic treatment. *Psychoanalytic Quarterly,* 1950, **19**, 482–500.

Alexander, F. Two forms of regression and their therapeutic implications. *Psychoanalytic Quarterly,* 1956, **25**, 256–275.

Alexander, F. *Science and psychoanalysis. Psychoanalytic Education for Practice.* Vol. 5. New York: Grune and Stratton, 1962: pp 176–177.

Alexander, F. *Evaluation of psychotherapy: evaluation of psychiatric treatment.* New York: Grune and Stratton, 1964.

Alexander, F. & French, T. *Psychoanalytic therapy.* New York: Ronald Press, 1946.

Alexander, F. & Selesnick, S. *The history of psychiatry.* New York: Harper & Row, 1966.

Arlow, J. A. & Brenner, C. The concept of regression and the structural theory. *Psychoanalytic Quarterly,* 1960, **29**, 89–103.

Bateson, G. & Ruesch, J. *Communication.* New York: W. W. Norton, 1951.

Benedek, T. Dynamics of the countertransference. *Bulletin of the Menninger Clinic,* 1953, **17**, 201–208.

Bion, W. R. On hallucination. *International Journal of Psycho-Analysis*, 1958, **39**, 341–349.

Blanck, G. & Blanck, R. *Ego psychology: Theory and Practice*. New York: Columbia University Press, 1974.

Bloch, D. Fantasy and the fear of infanticide. *Psychoanalytic Review*, 1974, **61**, 5–31.

Borosen, W. & Ginsberg, R. *The best of fact*. New York: Trident Press, 1967.

Boyer, L. B. Office treatment of schizophrenic patients by psychoanalysis. *The Psychoanalytic Forum*, 1966, **1**, 337–346.

Braatøy, T. *Fundamentals of psychoanalytic technique*. New York: John Wiley & Sons, 1954.

Braitwaite, R. B. *Scientific explanation*. New York: Harper Torchbooks, 1960.

Brenner, C. *An elementary textbook of psychoanalysis*. New York: Doubleday & Co., 1957.

Bronowski, J. *Science and human values*. New York: Harper Torchbooks, 1965.

Caligor, L., & Wittenberg, E. The interpersonal approach with particular emphasis on the obsessional. In B. Wolman (Ed.), *Psychoanalytic Techniques*. New York: Basic Books, 1967.

Chessick, R. D. Use of the couch in the psychotherapy of the borderline. *Archives of General Psychiatry*, 1971, **25**, 307–313.

Circot, J. E. *A dictionary of symbols*. New York: Philosophical Library, 1962.

Colby, K. *A primer for psychotherapists*. New York: Ronald Press, 1951.

Coltrera, J. T., & Ross, N. Freud's psychoanalytic technique—from the beginning to 1923. In B. Wolman (Ed.), *Psychoanalytic Techniques*. New York: Basic Books, 1967.

Dean, E. S. Drowsiness as a symptom of counter-transference. *Psychoanalytic Quarterly*, 1957, **26**, 246–247.

Dickes, R. The defensive function of an altered state of consciousness. *Journal of American Psychoanalytic Association*, 1965, **13**, 356–403.

Dosuzkov, T. Sleep during the psychoanalytic treatment: A case of conversion hysteria. *Psychoanalytic Review*, 1952, **39**, 339–344.

Eisendorfer, A. The selection of candidates applying for psychoanalytic training. *The Psychoanalytic Quarterly*, 1959, **28**, 374–378.

Ekstein, R. On current trends in psychoanalytic technique. In M. Lindner (Ed.), *Explorations in psychoanalysis*. (Essays in honor of Theodore Reik on the occasion of his sixty-fifth birthday, May 12, 1953.) New York: Julian Press, 1953.

Ellenberger, H. F. *The discovery of the unconscious*. New York: Basic Books, 1970.

Fairbairn, R. Nature and aims of treatment. *International Journal of Psycho-Analysis,* 1958, **34,** 374–385.

Farrow, E. *Psycho-analyze yourself.* New York: Lancer Books, 1953.

Fenichel, O. *The psychoanalytic theory of neurosis.* New York: W. W. Norton, Inc., 1945.

Ferenczi, S. (1919) *Further contributributions to the theory and technique of psychoanalysis. Vol. II. On the technique of psycho-analysis.* New York: Basic Books, 1952.

Ferenczi, S. (1920) *Further contributions to the theory and technique of psycho-analysis.* Vol. II. *The further development of an active therapy in psycho-analysis.* New York: Basic Books, 1952.

Ferenczi, S. (1926) *Further contributions to the theory and technique of psycho-analysis. Falling asleep during analysis.* Vol. II. New York: Basic Books, 1952.

Ferenczi, S. (1926) *Final Contributions to the Problems and Methods of Psycho-analysis,* Vol. III. New York: Basic Books, 1955.

Ferenczi, S. *Sex in psycho-analysis.* New York: Dover Publications, 1956.

Freud, A. *The psycho-analytic treatment of children.* London: Imago Publishing Co., 1946. (a)

Freud, A. *The ego and the mechanisms of defense.* New York: International Universities Press, 1946. (b)

Freud, A. Problems of technique in adult analysis. *Bulletin of the Philadelphia Association of Psychoanalysis,* 1954, **4,** 44–69.

Freud, S. (1888) Introduction to Bernheim. *Standard Edition,* 1961, **1,** 73–89.

Freud, S. (1889) Review of Forel. *Standard Edition,* 1961, **1,** 90–102.

Freud, S. (1891) Hypnosis. *Standard Edition,* 1961, **1,** 103–114.

Freud, S. (1892a) Preface and notes to J. M. Charcot Tuesday lectures. *Standard Edition,* 1961, **1,** 131–147.

Freud, S. (1892b) A case of successful treatment by hypnotism. *Standard Edition,* 1961, **1,** 115–130.

Freud, S. (1893) Charcot, *Standard Edition,* 1961, **3,** 9–24.

Freud, S. (1895) Studies in hysteria. *Standard Edition.* 1961, **2,** 1–343.

Freud, S. (1898) Sexuality in the aetiology of the neurosis. *Standard Edition,* 1963, **3,** 261–286.

Freud, S. (1900) The interpretation of dreams, *Standard Edition,* 1963, **4,** 1–630.

Freud, S. (1901) Autobiographical note. *Standard Edition,* 1961, **3,** 323–385.

Freud, S. (1904) Freud's psycho-analytic procedure. *Standard Edition,* 1961, **7,** 249–256.

Freud, S. (1905a) On psychotherapy. *Standard Edition,* 1961, **7,** 256–270.

Freud, S. (1905b) Jokes and their relation to the unconscious. *Standard Edition.* 1961, **8**:3–243.

Freud, S. (1912a) Recommendations to physician practising psychoanalysis. *Standard Edition,* 1961, **12**, 109–120.

Freud, S. (1912b) Totem and taboo. *Standard Edition,* 1963, **13**, 1–164.

Freud, S. (1913a) A difficulty in the path of psychoanalysis. *Standard Edition,* 1961, **17**, 135–144.

Freud, S. (1913b) On beginning the treatment (further recommendations in the technique of psychoanalysis). *Standard Edition,* 1961, **12**, 121–144.

Freud, S. (1914a) On the history of the psycho-analytic movement. *Standard Edition,* 1963, **14**, 3–66.

Freud, S. (1914b) On narcissism: an introduction. *Standard Edition,* 1963, **14**, 67–104.

Freud, S. (1915) The unconscious. *Standard Edition,* 1961, **14**, 159–204.

Freud, S. (1917a) On transformation of instinct as exemplified in anal erotism. *Standard Edition,* 1963, **17**, 125–134.

Freud, S. (1917b) A metapsychological supplement to the theory of dreams. *Standard Edition,* 1963, **14**, 219–236.

Freud, S. (1919) Lines of advance in psychoanalytic therapy. *Standard Edition,* 1961, **17**, 157–168.

Freud, S. (1925) An autobiographical study. *Standard Edition,* 1963, **20**, 3–76.

Freud, S. (1927a) The question of lay analysis. *Standard Edition,* 1963, **20**, 218–250.

Freud, S. (1927a) The future of an illusion. *Standard Edition,* 1963, **21**, 3–58.

Freud, S. (1927b) Postcript to discussion of lay analysis. *Standard Edition,* 1963, **20**, 59–158.

Freud, S. (1927) Inhibitions, symptoms, and anxiety. *Standard Edition,* 1961, **20**, 77–178.

Freud, S. (1930) Civilization and its discontents. *Standard Edition,* 1963, **21**, 59–158.

Freud, S. (1940) An outline of psychoanalysis. *Standard Edition,* 1963, **23**, 141–208.

Fromm-Reichmann, Frieda. *Principles of intensive psychotherapy.* Chicago: University of Chicago Press, 1950.

Gabe, S. Falling asleep during the analytic hour. *The Psychoanalytic Quarterly,* 1951, **20**, 344–345.

Gedo, J. & Pollock, G. The question of research in psychoanalytic technique. In B. Wolman (Ed.), *Psychoanalytic techniques.* New York: Basic Books, 1967.

Gordon, B. W., Glover, E., Brenner, A. K., Bromberg, N., & Sterling, H. *The psychoanalytic psychotherapy of adolescents.* Fifth Annual Scientific Conference on Psychoanalysis. New York: Council for Psychoanalytic Psychotherapy, 1967.

Goshen, C. E. (ed.) *Documentary history of psychiatry.* New York: Philosophical Library, 1967.

Greenacre, P. *Emotional growth.* Vol. II. New York: International Universities Press, 1971.

Greenacre, P. The role of transference: practical considerations in relation to psychoanalytic theory. (In) *Emotional growth.* Vol. II. New York: International Universities Press, 1971.

Greenson, R. *The technique and practice of psychoanalysis.* New York: International Universities Press, 1967. By permission of International Universities Press.

Grigson, J. Personal communication, 1976.

Grotjahn, M. *Beyond laughter.* New York: McGraw-Hill Book Company, 1957.

Gruen, A. The couch or the man. *The Psychoanalytic Review,* 1967, **54,** 72–79.

Guntrip, H. *Psychoanalytic theory, therapy, and the self.* New York: Basic Books, 1971.

Haak, N. Comments on the analytic situation. *International Journal of Psycho-Analysis,* 1957, **38,** 183–195.

Hall, M. H. A conversation with Henry A. Murray. *Psychology Today,* 1968, **2,** 56–63.

Hall, R. & Closson, W. An experimental study of the couch. *Journal of Nervous and Mental Disorders,* 1964, **138, 474–480.**

Halpern, S. Free association in 423 B.C. *The Psychoanalytic Review,* 1963, **50,** 419–435.

Harper, R. *Psychoanalysis and psychotherapy: 36 systems.* Englewood Cliffs, N.J.: Prentice-Hall, 1959.

Hirsch, P. *Never on freud day.* New York: Pyramid Books, 1968.

Hollander, M. *The Practice of psychoanalytic psychotherapy.* New York: Grune & Stratton, 1965.

Hunt, M., Corman, R., & Ormont, L. R. *The talking cure.* New York: Harper & Row, 1954.

Isakower, O. A contribution to the patho-psychology of phenomena associated with falling asleep. *International Journal of Psycho-Analysis,* 1936, **19,** 331–345.

Jekels, L. A bioanalytical contribution to the problem of sleep and wakefulness. *Psychoanalytic Quarterly,* 1945, **14,** 169–189.

Jones, E. (Ed.) The Collected Papers of Sigmund Freud. *The life and work of Sigmund Freud.* Vol. I. New York: Basic Books, 1953. From THE

COLLECTED PAPERS OF SIGMUND FREUD, Volume I (2) edited by Ernest Jones, M.D., authorized translation under the supervision of Joan Riviere, Published by Basic Books, Inc., publishers, New York, by arrangement with The Hogarth Press Ltd. and The Institute of Psychoanalysis, London.

Jones, E. (Ed.) The Collected Papers of Sigmund Freud. *The life and work of Sigmund Freud.* Vol. II. New York: Basic Books, 1955. From THE COLLECTED PAPERS OF SIGMUND FREUD, Volume I (2) edited by Ernest Jones, M.D., authorized translation under the supervision of Joan Riviere, Published by Basic Books, Inc., publishers, New York, by arrangement with The Hogarth Press Ltd. and The Institute of Psychoanalysis, London.

Junge, K. Personal communication, 1976.

Kanzer, M. & Blum, H. P. Classical psychoanalysis since 1939. In B. Wolman (Ed.), *Psychoanalytic Techniques.* New York: Basic Books, 1967.

Kelman, H. The use of the analytic couch. *American Journal of Psychoanalysis,* 1954, **14**, 65–82.

Kelman, H. & Vollmerhansen, J. W. On Karen Horney's psychoanalytic techniques: developments and perspectives. In B. Wolman (Ed.), *Psychoanalytic Techniques.* New York: Basic Books, 1967.

Khan, M. Dream psychology and the evolution of the psychoanalytic situation. *International Journal of Psycho-Analysis,* 1962, **43**, 21–31.

Klein, M. *The psychoanalysis of children.* London: Hogarth Press, 1954.

Kline, M. V. *Freud and hypnosis.* New York: Julian Press, 1958.

Knapp, P. H. The ear, listening, and hearing. In S. Lorand (Ed.), *The yearbook of psychoanalysis.* New York: International Universities Press, 1954.

Kohut, H. *The analysis of the self: a systematic approach to the psychoanalytic treatment of narcissistic personality disorders.* New York: International Universities Press, 1971.

Kris, E. Ego psychology: Interpretation in psychoanalytic therapy. *Psychoanalytic Quarterly,* 1951, **20**, 15–30.

Kris, E. *Psychoanalytic explorations in art.* New York: International Universities Press, 1952.

Kubie, L. *Practical and theoretical aspects of psychoanalysis.* New York: International Universities Press, 1950.

Leboyer, F. *Birth without violence.* New York: Alfred A. Knopf, 1973.

Lewin, B. *Selected writings of Bertram D. Lewin.* New York: Psychoanalytic Quarterly, 1973.

Little, R. B. Spider phobias. *Psychoanalytic Quarterly,* 1967, **36**, 51–60.

Lorand, S. *Clinical studies in psychoanalysis,* New York: International Universities Press, 1950.

Lorand, S. Reflections on the development of psychoanalysis in New York from 1925. *The International Journal of Psychoanalysis,* 1969, **50,** 589–595.

Macalpine, I. The development of transference. *Psychoanalytic Quarterly,* 1950, **19,** 501–539.

Marmor, J. A re-evaluation of certain aspects of psychoanalytic theory and practice. In L. Salzman & J. H. Masserman (Eds.), *Modern concepts of psychoanalysis.* New York: Philosophical Library, 1962.

Mellinger, B. Personal communication, 1976.

Menninger, K. *Theory of psychoanalytic technique.* New York: Basic Books, 1958.

Miller, G. On turning psychology over to the unwashed. *Psychology Today,* 1969, **3,** 110–198.

Millett, J. The changing faces of psychoanalytic training. In L. Salzman & J. H. Masserman (Eds.), *Modern concepts of psychoanalysis.* New York: Philosophical Library, Inc., 1962.

Moser, T. *Years of Apprenticeship On The Couch,* New York: Urizen Books, 1977.

Nelson, B. Self-images and systems of spiritual direction in the history of European civilization. In S. Z. Klausher (Ed.), *The quest for self-control: classical philosophies and scientific research.* New York: Free Press, 1965.

Parkin, S. Emergence of sleep during psychoanalysis: A clinical note. *International Journal of Psycho-Analysis,* 1955, **36,** 174–176.

Perls, F. *Gestalt therapy verbatim.* Lafayette, Ca: Real People Press, 1969.

Racker, H. The meanings and uses of countertransference. *Psychoanalytic Quarterly,* 1957, **26,** 303–357.

Redlich, F. & Bingham, J. *The inside story.* New York: Vintage Books, 1953.

Reich, W. *Character analysis.* New York: Orgone Institute Press, 1949.

Reik, T. *Listening with the third ear.* New York: Grove Press, 1948.

Roazen, P. *Freud and his followers.* New York: Alfred A. Knopf, Inc., 1975.

Robertiello, R. C. The couch. *Psychoanalytic Review,* 1967, **54,** 69–71.

Rosenbaum, S. Symbolic meaning and theoretical significance of the analytic couch. *Science and Psychoanalysis,* 1967, **11,** 182–201.

Rosenfeld, H. Transference-phenomena and transference-analysis in an acute catatonic schizophrenic patient. *International Journal of Psycho-Analysis,* 1952, **33,** 457–464.

Saul, L. *Technic and practice of psychoanalysis.* Philadelphia: J. B. Lippen-cott, 1958.

Schafer, R. Content analysis in the Rorschach test. In R. P. Knight & C. R. Friedman (Eds.), *Psychoanalytic psychiatry and psychology.* New York: International Universities Press, 1954.

Scott, W. C. Patients who sleep or look at the psychoanalyst during treatment. *International Journal of Psycho-Analysis,* 1952, **33,** 465–469.

Scott, W. C. Sleep in psychoanalysis. *Bulletin of the Philadelphia Association for Psychoanalysis,* 1956, **6,** 72–83.

Scott, W. C. Personal communication, 1971.

Selesnick, S. T. The techniques of psychoanalysis developed by Franz Alexander and Thomas French. In B. Wolman (Ed.), *Psychoanalytic techniques.* New York: Basic Books, 1967.

Sharpe, E. F. Technique of psychoanalysis. In *Collected Papers on Psychoanalysis.* Vol. I. London: Hogarth Press, 1950.

Sherwood, M. *Logic of explanation in psychoanalysis.* New York: Academic Press, 1969.

Shields, R. The too-good mother. *International Journal of Psycho-Analysis,* 1964, **45,** 85–88.

Shur, M. The ego and the id in anxiety. In *The psychoanalytic study of the child.* New York: International Universities Press, 1958.

Simmel, E. Contribution to symposium on neurotic disturbances of sleep. *International Journal of Psycho-Analysis,* 1942, **23,** 65–68.

Smith, B. Personal communication, 1976.

Spitz, R. Transference: The analytical setting and its prototype. *International Journal of Psycho-Analysis,* 1956, **37,** 380–385.

Spotnitz, H. *The Couch and the circle.* New York: Alfred A. Knopf, 1961.

Spotnitz, H. Techniques for the resolution of the narcissistic defense. In B. Wolman (Ed.), *Psychoanalytic techniques.* New York: Basic Books, 1967.

Spotnitz, H. *Modern psychoanalysis of the schizophrenic patient.* New York: Grune & Stratton, 1969. By permission of Grune & Stratton, Inc., © 1969.

Spotnitz, H. *Psychotherapy of preoedipal conditions: Schizophrenia and severe character disorders.* New York: Jason Aronson, 1976.

Stein, A. & Tarachow, S. Psychoanalytic psychotherapy. In B. Wolman (Ed.), *Psychoanalytic Techniques.* New York: Basic Books, 1967.

Stern, H. The truth as a resistance to free association. *Psychoanalytic Review,* 1966, **53,** 142–146.

Stern, H. & Wilson, B. Use of the couch in psychoanalysis, a dialogue. 1974 (unpublished paper).

Stone, L. Transference, sleep in a neurosis with duodenalulcer. *International Journal of Psycho-Analysis,* 1947, **28,** 18–32.

Thompson, C. *Psychoanalysis: it's evolution and development.* New York: Hermitage House, 1950.

Waelder, R. *Basic theory of psychoanalysis.* New York: Shocken Books, 1964.

Wolman, B. B. (Ed.) Psychoanalytic Techniques. *A Handbook for the Practicing Psychoanalyst,* New York: Basic Books, Inc., Publishers, 1976. © 1976.

Wolf-Man. *The wolf-man.* New York: Basic Books, 1971.

Zilboorg, G. & Henry, G. W. *A history of medical psychology.* New York: W. W. Norton, 1941.

Zubek, J. P., & MacNeill, M. Perceptual deprivation phenomena: role of the recumbent position. *Journal of Abnormal Psychology,* 1967, **72,** 147–150.

Zuckerman, M., Persky, H., Link, K. E., & Basu, G. K. Experimental and social factors determining responses to sensory deprivation, social isolation, and confinement. *Journal of Abnormal Psychology,* 1968, **73,** 183–194.

Acting Out, 136, 137
Activity, 27
Analytic setting, 123, 137-142, 188
Analytic Training, 169-170

Character traits, 135-136
Consciousness, 64, 110
Couch, 50, 55, 56, 59, 91, 92, 94, 102, 117-120, 124, 129, 138, 142, 152, 172, 177, 180, 191-192
Counter transference, 90, 103, 129, 130

Defiance, as resistance, 28
Denial, 14, 15
Dependency, 21
Depression, 113
Displacement, 14, 15
Dreams, 91

Ego, 15, 66, 127, 162
Exhibitionism, 31, 113-114

Free association, 82, 83, 183
Frequency of analytic sessions, 191

Humor, 20, 39, 44, 51
Hypnosis, 44, 59, 77, 90
Hypnotherapy, 77, 78, 79, 80, 81, 93, 124
Hysteria, 78, 79, 108

Inferiority, 24, 54
Introjection, 29
Isolation, 14, 15

Jokes, 39, 40, 41, 45, 46, 47
Judgment, 16

Listening, 16, 32
Looking, 21, 29, 30, 84, 97

Memory, 16

Oral tradition, 61, 176

Passivity, 24, 26, 27, 107, 185
Perception, 16
Physiological functioning, 105, 107
Projection, 29, 115
Psychosis, 25, 143

Rationalization, 18
Recumbent position, 61, 62, 107, 111
Relaxation, 21, 34, 77, 78, 79, 80, 82, 144
Repression, 14, 15, 77
Resistance, 26, 76, 87, 111, 114, 126, 127, 132, 134, 155, 162
Resistance solvent (strategy), 128, 137-138, 156, 158, 160, 163, 164, 166

Schizophrenic, 85, 87, 145, 150, 154
Secondary gain, 166
Sexuality, 41, 42, 48
Shame, 31
Sleep, 80, 87, 88, 89, 94, 95, 96, 99, 101, 102, 103
Sublimation, 16
Superego, 42, 43
Superiority, 24, 35, 54
Symbol, 36, 55, 56, 147, 182
Symbolic, 20, 83

Training analysis, 57, 60
Transference, 76, 115, 164, 174, 183

Unconscious, 75, 79

Abraham, Karl, 70
Adler, Alfred, 24, 69, 70
Adler, Gerhard, 25, 36, 199
Adler, Kurt, 24, 199
Ahsen, Akter, 24, 27
Alexander, Franz, 59, 79, 171, 194, 196, 200
Aristophanes, 59
Arlow, Jacob A., 74, 79

Bateson, Gregory, 29, 199
Benedek, Teresa, 130
Bernheim, Henri, 61, 63, 65, 195
Bingham, J., 200
Bion, Wilfred, R., 80-81, 199
Blanck, Gertrude, 152-153
Blanck, Rubin, 152, 153-154
Bloch, Dorothy, 176
Blum, Harold P., 188, 200
Borosen, William, 47, 200
Boyer, Bruce L., 143-144, 173, 199
Braatoy, Trygve, 105-108, 120-121, 140-141, 151-152, 186, 196, 197, 198
Bratwaite, R.B., 189
Brenner, Charles, 15, 74
Breuer, Josef, 61, 62, 195
Bronowski, Jacob, 189
Brucke, Ernst, 195

Caligor, Leopold, 144-145, 199
Charcot, J.M., 61, 62, 63, 195
Chessick, Richard D., 14, 130-131, 145-146, 153-154, 173, 197, 199
Circot, J.E., 36, 199
Closson, W.G., Jr., 14, 172, 196
Colby, Kenneth, 153
Coltrera, Joseph T., 30, 65, 196
Corman, Rena, 127

Dean, Edward S., 90
Dickes, Robert, 89-90
Dosuzkov, Theodore, 88

Eisendorfer, Arnold, 30
Ellenberger, Henri F., 194

Fairbairn, Ronald, 178
Farrow, E. Pickworth, 117
Fenichel, Otto, 31, 74
Ferenczi, Sandor, 34, 69, 86, 100, 101, 117, 198
Forel, August, 195
Freud, Anna, 15, 74, 78, 144, 197, 199, 200
Freud, Sigmund, 14, 18, 19, 21, 23, 30, 34, 37, 39, 44, 45, 48, 49, 57, 61, 62, 64, 170, 197, 198, 199
Fromm, Erich, 68
Fromm-Reichmann, Frieda, 19, 68, 98, 142, 186, 187, 198

Gabe, Sigmund, 87
Gedo, John, 66, 75, 196
Ginsburg, Ralph, 47, 200
Glover, Edward, 190
Gordon, Bernice W., 142
Goshen, Charles E., 194
Greenacre, Phyllis, 83, 123-124, 198
Greenson, Ralph, 31, 127, 129, 132, 135, 198, 199
Grigson, Joyce, 154-155
Grotjahn, Martin, 41, 199
Gruen, Arno, 14, 179-180, 197, 200
Guntrip, Harry, 121, 198

Haak, Nils, 82-83, 143
Hall, Mary H., 14, 189
Hall, Robert A., 172, 196
Halpern, Sidney, 43, 194
Harper, Robert, 38
Hartmann, Heinz, 74
Henry, G.W., 194
Hirsch, P., 41
Hollander, Marc, 131-132, 191, 201
Holt, Robert, 11
Horney, Karen, 19, 68, 122
Hunt, Morton, 127

Isakower, Otto, 87

Jekels, Ludwig, 87
Jones, Ernest, 68, 76, 77, 78, 196, 197
Jung, Carl, 36, 68
Junge, Kyra, 144

Kanzer, Mark, 188, 200
Kelman, Harold, 14, 19, 122, 141-142, 196, 198
Khan, Masud, 83
Klein, Melenie, 144, 199
Kline, Milton, U. 44, 194
Knapp, Peter H., 32
Kohut, Heinz, 127
Kris, Ernst, 71, 74, 79, 82, 197
Kubie, Lawrence, 161-162, 169

Leboyer, F., 33, 34
Lewin, Bertram, 86, 87, 90-94, 169-170, 198
Liebout, 61
Little, Ralph, B., 35
Lorand, Sandor, 19, 72
Lowenstein, Rudolph, 74

Macalpine, Ida, 86
MacNeill, M., 81, 198
Marmor, Judd, 174-175, 200
Mellinger, Barry, 127

Menninger, Karl, 84-85, 99-100
Miller, George, 52, 53
Millett, John, 72, 196
Moser, Tilmann, 35, 36, 73, 84-84
Murray, Henry, 187, 201

Nelson, Benjamin, 188

Ormont, Louis R., 127

Parkin, Alan, 89
Perls, Fritz, 102, 198
Pfister, Oscar, 71
Pollock, George H., 66, 75, 196

Racker, Heinrich, 103
Rank, Otto, 68
Redlich, Fritz, 46, 47, 200
Reich, Wilhelm, 68, 110-111, 141, 197
Reik, Theodore, 15, 71, 99, 129
Roazen, Paul, 65, 66, 70, 71, 74, 75, 129-130, 191-192, 196, 200
Robertiello, Richard C., 14, 179, 189, 196, 200
Rosenbaum, Salo, 14, 140, 197
Rosenfeld, Herbert, 103
Ross, Nathanial, 30, 65, 196
Ruesch, Jurgen, 29, 199

Sachs, Hans, 71
Saul, Leon, 144, 199
Schafer, Roy, 79
Scott, William C., 88-89
Selesnick, Shelden T., 59, 171, 194, 196
Sharpe, Ella Freeman, 16, 32, 199
Sherwood, Michael, 56
Shields, Robert W., 83
Shur, Max, 78-79, 196, 197
Simmel, Ernst, 87
Smith, Barbera, 149
Socrates, 59, 194
Spitz, Rene, 83, 86

Spotnitz, Hyman, 25, 35, 103, 113, 120, 127, 132, 134-135, 137, 143, 155, 175, 176, 198, 199
Stein, Aaron, 122
Stekel, Wilhelm, 68, 69
Stern, Harold, 112, 180
Sullivan, Harry S., 19, 68
Szasz, Thomas, 199

Tarachow, Sidney, 122
Thompson, Clara, 65, 68, 194

Vollmerhansen, Joseph, 122-123

Waelder, Robert, 34, 75, 198
Wilson, Bradford, 180-182
Wittenberg, Rudolph, 144-145, 199
Wolf-Man, 67, 196

Zilboorg, Gregory, 194
Zubek, Joseph P., 81, 198
Zuckerman, Marcia, 61